THE CONTEMPORARY
AMERICAN NOVEL IN CONTEXT

Texts and Contexts
Series Editors: Gail Ashton and Fiona McCulloch

Texts and Contexts is a series of clear, concise and accessible introductions to key literary fields and concepts. The series provides the
literary, critical, historical context for texts and authors in a specific
literary area in a way that introduces a range of work in the field and
enables further independent study and reading.

Other titles available in the series:

Medieval English Romance in Context
Gail Ashton

Postcolonial Literatures in Context
Julie Mullaney

The Victorian Novel in Context
Grace Moore

THE CONTEMPORARY AMERICAN NOVEL IN CONTEXT

ANDREW DIX, BRIAN JARVIS AND PAUL JENNER

continuum

Continuum International Publishing Group

The Tower Building
11 York Road
London SE1 7NX

80 Maiden Lane, Suite 704
New York
NY 10038

www.continuumbooks.com

British Library Cataloguing-in-Publication Data
A catalogue record for this book is available from the British Library.

ISBN: 978-0-8264-1969-9 (hardback)
978-0-8264-3696-2 (paperback)

Library of Congress Cataloguing-in-Publication Data
A catalog record for this book is available from the Library of Congress.

Typeset by Fakenham Prepress Solutions, Fakenham, Norfolk NR21 8NN
Printed and bound in India

CONTENTS

ACKNOWLEDGEMENTS

For their enthusiastic response to our project from its inception, and their helpfulness and warmth during its completion, we are grateful to the series editors, Gail Ashton and Fiona McCulloch. Many thanks are due also to Colleen Coalter at Continuum.

A number of people have advised, sustained and cajoled us in our work on this book, and we wish to thank in particular Yuko Akiyama, Karen Kennedy and Clare, Bethany and Hannah Jarvis. We acknowledge, too, our students in the Department of English and Drama, Loughborough University: many of the book's ideas were first tested in lively seminar discussions, especially on the M.A. module *The American Novel Now*. Our intellectual debts to other critics working on contemporary American fiction will become apparent as the text unfolds.

SERIES EDITORS' PREFACE

Texts and Contexts offers clear and accessible introductions to key literary fields. Each book in the series outlines major historical, social, cultural and literary contexts that impact upon its specified area. It engages contemporary responses to selected texts and authors through a variety of exemplary close readings, by exploring the ideas of seminal theorists and/or a range of critical approaches, as well as examining adaptations and afterlives. Readers are encouraged to make connections and ground further independent study through 'Review, Reading and Research' sections at the end of each chapter which offer selected bibliographies, web resources, open and closed questions, discussion topics and pointers for extended research.

Note on the text

Where a work is discussed in a general context the date given is that of its first publication. Where extracts are quoted, the date given is that of the edition from which the extracts were taken. The bibliographic entry refers to the edition from which the extracts are quoted, and the date of first publication is given in brackets.

PART ONE

CONTEXTS

CHAPTER ONE

'WHO ARE WE?': SOCIAL AND CULTURAL CONTEXTS OF THE CONTEMPORARY AMERICAN NOVEL

INTRODUCTION

Sydney Smith, English critic and clergyman (1771–1845), once asked: 'Who reads an American book?' Noted for colourful pronouncements such as describing his idea of heaven as eating *pâté de foie gras* to the sound of trumpets, Smith was a professional eccentric whose literary xenophobia might seem easily dismissed. But at the time he asked it, in 1820, his scornful question was reflective less of personal idiosyncrasy than of solidified critical opinion. Compared with the long-established literatures of England, France, Germany and other European centres, that of the United States was universally seen as weak and malnourished. US literary independence was considered to lag well behind the nation's political liberation from the powers of Old Europe. By the middle of the nineteenth century, however, pioneering writers such as the novelist Herman Melville, the poet Walt Whitman and the critic Ralph Waldo Emerson had challenged any notion of cultural subservience and had begun both to theorize and to produce a distinctively American literature. Global literary trade has since become thoroughly equalized, with texts by US writers like Mark Twain, F. Scott Fitzgerald and J. D. Salinger travelling as widely as those by Europeans like Charles Dickens, Marcel Proust and George Orwell. To Smith's question, now, the likeliest answer is: 'Everybody'. And, of the varieties of 'American book' read in our time, few have greater prestige and circulation than the nation's contemporary novels.

This book offers a critical introduction to developments in the American novel from 1980 to 2010. Setting aside, regretfully, the innovative work done during this period by such US specialists of the short story form as Harold Brodkey, Raymond Carver and Lorrie Moore, we focus upon the production of longer fiction. Our primary aims are to communicate a sense of this body of work's formal and thematic richness and to explore important cultural and ideological questions which it raises. The book's middle chapters, from 3 to 6, ground the project by detailed study of four major preoccupations or tendencies in recent American fiction. Chapters 7 and 8, by contrast, are broader in focus, assessing first the afterlives of contemporary US novels in other media ranging from film adaptations to videogames, and second the strengths and weaknesses of various conceptual models by which this fiction might be interpreted. While we make no claims of definitiveness, we hope to have provided, by the end of the book, a cross-sectional view of significant novelistic production in the United States during the past thirty years.

We begin with two contextualizing chapters. Chapter 2 presents an overview of the state of contemporary US fiction, describing the novel's continuing abundance and variety and yet registering a sense of crisis in the form's cultural power, felt not only by advocates of newer visual and digital media but also by a number of American novelists themselves. Debates about the novel's status in the advanced mediascape of the United States today thus comprise a backdrop against which our case studies in the middle chapters are played out. In the present chapter, however, we offer not so much literary history as what Twain called 'historical history': a survey of political, economic and cultural tendencies in the US from Ronald Reagan's election as the 40th President in 1980 to the second year of Barack Obama's incumbency in 2010. The following sections identify major developments in the nation's internal organization and external disposition that are contexts for the novels discussed in this book.

The rise and fall of the American economy

During Bill Clinton's successful bid for the US presidency in 1992, a poster was prominently displayed in his campaign headquarters in Little Rock, Arkansas. 'The economy, stupid', it read, reminding campaigners of the theme they should consistently prioritize. Without suggesting that our readers need such forceful direction as Clinton staffers, we want, in similar vein, to underline the salience of the economy when thinking about the contemporary American novel. For while it is true that economics figures among the specialist knowledge of relatively few current novelists, the expansion, contraction, transformation and distribution of money in the United States between 1980 and the 2010 constitute, nevertheless, the chief structuring force upon the national life explored by their fiction.

As we write, the prospects for the US economy, and for Western capitalism more broadly, are deeply uncertain. Before describing the contemporary crisis, however, it is important to acknowledge its origins in the free-market economics administered at the start of our period by President Reagan. 'Reaganomics' – dubbed 'voodoo economics' by George Bush, Sr., before his service as Reagan's Vice-President – had as its operating principles a massive scaling-back of government spending (other than on defence and the prison system) and a correspondingly huge opening-up of opportunities to private capital. With markets deregulated and labour unions neutered, a green light was given to capitalistic activity, including investments of the most speculative kind. Enriching the lexicon (as well as high-flying corporate executives), Reaganomics saw the flourishing of *junk bonds* (high-yielding but high-risk forms of stock) and *leveraged buy-outs* (frequently predatory acquisitions of companies by financial conglomerates). Wall Street financiers were prominent among the period's *dramatis personae*, as in novels such as Tom Wolfe's *The Bonfire of the Vanities* (1987), with its megalomaniacal bond trader protagonist. Bret Easton Ellis's *American Psycho* (1991), a text we discuss in Chapter 3, is self-consciously an historical novel about this period, its catalogues of intoxicated consumption by Wall Street supermen both reproducing and, by virtue of their nauseous extravagance, resisting the ethos of Reaganomics.

Donald Pease suggests that US economic and social policy has, for decades, been designed to produce a 'consumer compound' (2009: 169), a space in which the nation's population is configured less as citizens than as bundles of appetites to be tickled by merchandisers. Yet such figures as the dispossessed African American killed by Patrick Bateman in *American Psycho* or the impoverished Mexican immigrant knocked down by a wealthy white Californian in T. C. Boyle's *The Tortilla Curtain* (1995) testify that the United States also houses immiserized, non-consuming classes. One radical study concludes that 'poverty is racialized and gendered in America' (Grosfoguel, Maldonado-Torres and Saldívar 2005: 15). Such a claim risks implying the universality of white affluence: the white working-class in the US has, after all, been badly hit by the collapse of traditional manufacturing, or by its outsourcing to overseas locales. Illustrative of the racial unevenness of access to American abundance, however, are figures released by the US Census Bureau in 2008, disclosing that while 11.2 per cent of whites counted as below the poverty line, the figures for Hispanics and African Americans were 23.2 percent and 24.7 percent respectively.

In the Clinton presidency, from 1993 to 2001, 'the US economy entered its longest period of expansion, unemployment fell to historic lows, inflation bottomed out' (Duncan and Goddard 2009: 32). While that era's prosperity was, as noted, unequally distributed, the mood-music was optimistic, in marked contrast to the sense of economic catastrophe that prevailed a decade later during the dying days of George W. Bush's administration. The autumn of 2008 saw scenes of fiscal trauma in the US unparalleled since the Wall Street Crash of 1929. A crisis in the supply of money was precipitated by the failure of such wantonly speculative schemes as *derivatives* (trading, without security, in the hope of assets' future increase in value) and *sub-prime lending* (advancing mortgages to ill-equipped borrowers). Gigantic finance corporations, from Lehman Brothers to AIG, entered variously into bankruptcy or into (temporary and partial) public ownership. At the time of writing, it is still unclear whether the massive programme for economic renewal engineered by President Obama will prevent the US from entering a second recession.

Writing before the current crisis of American money, the social theorist Immanuel Wallerstein argued that the US is doomed to lose global pre-eminence in the twenty-first century. His book, *The Decline of American Power* (2003), suggests that an atrophying of America's military muscle will accompany the collapse of its capitalistic power in the face of emerging economies such as China, India and Brazil. On the other hand, the US is still the greatest of economic powerhouses, its gross domestic product standing at $14.6 trillion in 2010 (compared with $2.7 trillion in 1980). Evidently, then, the current condition and future trajectory of the United States economy are open to debate. This is a conversation in which the nation's novelists, as well as its academics, may participate.

While corporate finance has a technical complexity and arithmetical aridity not immediately appealing to writers of fiction, there are important counter-examples. Don DeLillo's *Cosmopolis* (2003), studied in Chapter 6, offers dark reflections on the 'dotcom bubble', that explosion of internet-based commerce at the very end of the twentieth century. Currently, we may also be seeing the emergence of 'the credit crunch novel' dedicated to measuring the effects of 'toxic' debt on the emotional, cultural and ideological health of the US. Prominent examples of this new sub-genre are Adam Haslett's *Union Atlantic* and Jonathan Dee's *The Privileges*, both published in 2010.

Culture wars

Take a look at a map of the United States that has been colour-coded to reflect the typical performances of Democrats and Republicans in presidential elections since 1980. Reversing the chromatic conventions of UK politics, red in this cartography stands for the conservative Republicans, blue for the liberally inclined Democrats. Red is seen to stain the map in the Rocky Mountains, across much of the Mid-west and throughout the Confederacy's old heartlands in the South. Democrat blue dyes the map in areas frequently of lesser geographical scale but greater population density: the Pacific coast, Mid-western enclaves around the Great Lakes, and the entirety of New England. Electoral cartography of this kind is, of course, highly schematic: disenfranchised Democrats exist in redneck domains in Texas, just as unhappy Republicans can be found inhabiting ultra-liberal Massachusetts. Nevertheless, the distinction between what have come to be called *red states* and *blue states* is striking, and stands for divisions in the country that are not simply party-political but deeply cultural.

Currently in progress, according to the conservative political scientist Samuel Huntington, is a 'war over the nature of American national identity' (2004: 142). Although new fronts open up daily in this conflict, certain battle-lines can be clearly discerned. For US conservatives, the many agents of 'de-Americanization' include advocates of gun control; atheists, agnostics and adherents of non-Christian religions; teachers of evolutionary biology, as against creationism; supporters of women's right to abortion, along with other feminist advances; campaigners for gay and lesbian equality;

primary speakers of languages other than English; theorists of multiculturalism; and representatives of identity politics of all kinds (excepting, of course, those representing the cause of the ethnically white). In *Who Are We?* (2004), his attempt to repair what he identifies as an 'eroded Americanism' (8), Huntington goes so far as to argue that the speaking of English, the foregrounding of European artistic and philosophical traditions, and the privileging of Christianity (especially Protestantism) constitute the nation's 'core culture', a social adhesive potentially stronger than, say, US citizens' shared, abstract commitment to the system of liberal democracy.

In developing this model of core culture, Huntington is anxious to deny that it is the property of any single race or ethnicity. When he refers to the abiding value of 'Anglo-Protestant culture', he says he is giving the term 'Anglo' 'only a cultural and not an ethnic meaning' (2004: 301). Unsurprisingly, however, this fragile distinction collapses, and a sense of white privilege often returns with a vengeance in *Who Are We?* Resembling an 'ideologue of an empire that is declining' (Grosfoguel, Maldonado-Torres and Saldívar 2005: 17), Huntington identifies multicultural communities in general, and Latino/as in particular, as a threat to the social and, ultimately, the territorial integrity of the United States. Latino/as incite his most phobic prose, given their high numbers (forecast to comprise 25 percent of the population by 2060), their residual speaking of Spanish as first language, their preference for congregating in particular areas rather than dispersing across the US, and their occupation, like a reconquering army, of lands in the South-west that once belonged to Mexico. As well as being disputed by many academics, however, Huntington's attempt to freeze development of the United States in the interests of traditional white authority is countered by much of the nation's recent fiction. In Chapter 4, we discuss Toni Morrison's African American uncovering of the catastrophe of white hegemony in *Beloved* (1987); while in Chapters 5 and 6 we consider novels in which the intersections of the US with non-white demographics and with alien cultures are construed, at least partially, as liberating.

If these 'culture wars' have multiple locations, they also have varying intensities. The contests over American values are not fought out merely in the regulated discourse of electoral politics; nor are they straightforwardly reducible to a struggle between

Republican and Democrat. At the time of writing, for example, the rightward edge of US politics is being redesigned by the American Tea Party Movement, founded in 2009 in protest against the scale of Obama's public spending on healthcare reform and economic renewal. Named after a key moment in the struggle against British colonial rule in 1773, and thereby implicitly trying to resuscitate a white-dominated America as if subsequent multicultural history had not happened, the Tea Party is not simply driving mainstream Republicanism to the right but is also partially displacing it. The movement's sentiments, as voiced by figures like talk radio host Rush Limbaugh and ultra-conservatism's poster-girl Sarah Palin, are not so far from political sedition. A notable fact, indeed, about the period covered by this book is the emergence of a militant right wing in the US prepared to resort to separatist gestures, even to violence, in order to defend its understanding of the nation's core values. The right's recent martyrology embraces such figures as Randy Weaver, who conducted an armed standoff with FBI agents at Ruby Ridge, Idaho in 1992 and the militiaman Timothy McVeigh, who bombed the Alfred P. Murrah Federal Building in Oklahoma City in 1995, causing 168 deaths.

At present, there is no sign of any cessation of hostilities in the US culture wars. The summer of 2010 saw tensions between supporters and opponents of the planned siting of an Islamic community centre, several blocks from the consecrated space of Ground Zero in Manhattan, that were indicative of the unpredictability of the times and places of such cultural skirmishing. Writing before Barack Obama's arrival in the White House, Pease optimistically suggested that because of his complex ethnicity and acculturation he might be a figure able to manage differences between 'multiple constituencies' (2009: 213), to serve as 'the placeholder for all who could not be included within the social order' (210). The opposite, of course, has proven to be the case. Right-wing dissenters have been vividly aggrieved not simply by Obama's commitment of significant federal resources to fields like healthcare but by his cultural repertoire itself. This President, it is safe to say, does not share his predecessor George W. Bush's demotic taste for horseshoe-pitching; he is more likely to be found looking at abstract art or, suggestively for us, reading his country's contemporary fiction.

In the ongoing battles over the culture of the United States, it may seem as if the voices of placard-wavers, internet campaigners, bloggers, Fox TV pundits and talk radio broadcasters sound the loudest. Yet this endowing of the cultural realm with high value also opens up opportunities for American novelists. Specialists, after all, in teasing out the significance of social symbols and rituals, adept at uncovering and exploring fantasies and phobias, they are well placed to participate in the struggle for the meaning of the US. Contemporary writers of fiction imaginatively affiliated to the Tea Party, and to the American right generally, are hard to identify, it is true, other than in popular genres like the conspiracy thriller. However, novelists variously associated with liberal and radical perspectives figure in our case studies in Chapters 3 to 6, their texts not simply reports from afar on 'the US cultural imaginary' (Dawson and Schueller 2007: 2) but active contributions to its making.

The United States in the world

'The past is never dead,' writes William Faulkner, eminent novelist of the American South, in *Requiem for a Nun* (1951). 'It's not even past.' While our emphasis in this book is on the new in the United States since 1980, that should not be taken to imply that the nation has been forgetful of history during this time. On the contrary, retellings of traumatic periods in the life of America continue to appear, not least in novel form: Sherman Alexie's recapitulation of Indian genocide in *Reservation Blues* (1995), for example, or Edward P. Jones's narrativization of slavery in Virginia in *The Known World* (2003). Less dead than most of the pre-1980 American past, however, is a trauma experienced, at least partially, beyond the nation's borders: namely, US involvement in the Vietnam War of the 1960s and early 1970s, that forlorn attempt to resist the spread of Communist rule in South-east Asia which cost the lives of 58,000 American service personnel and several million Vietnamese combatants and civilians, as well as leaving ecological ruin and, back home, a disorienting sensation of military defeat. American novelists have followed film-makers in reflecting on both the attrition of soldiering in Vietnam and the war's devastating impact on the home front. Exponents of such fiction from earlier in our period include Jayne Anne Phillips in *Machine Dreams* (1984), Bobbie Ann Mason in *In Country* (1985) and Tim O'Brien in a significant body of work from the 1970s onwards that extends to *In the Lake of the Woods* (1994) and *July, July* (2002). That US culture is still, to some extent, fashioned in the shadow of this war is suggested by the continuing attention given 'the Vietnam novel', notable recent examples being Denis Johnson's *Tree of Smoke* (2007) and Karl Marlantes's *Matterhorn* (2010).

For John Carlos Rowe, US representations of Vietnam have not, ultimately, amounted to a chastening reflection on national guilt and a prospectus for a new kind of American involvement in the world. He suggests, instead, that the effect of 'a wide range of media', not excluding the novel, has been to turn 'the renarrativization of a military and colonial failure into a foundation for subsequent military ventures' (Rowe 2007: 45). While Vietnam signalled, in psychosexual terms, a kind of emasculation of the US, the heavily militarized Reagan era indeed saw the restoration of national potency. Avoiding large-scale armed campaigns, Reagan instead 'supplied spectatorial publics with representative heroic actions' (Pease 2009: 64), such as invading Grenada in 1983 and bombing Libya in 1986. A pattern was established of massive deployment of highly technologized weaponry against low-tech, often modestly numbered enemies. This model was adhered to by Reagan's successor, George Bush, Sr.: first during the invasion of Panama in 1989, then – appropriately scaled-up, given the larger opposing army – during the First Gulf War against Iraq in 1991 (waged to relieve illegally occupied Kuwait, thus safeguarding US commercial and geopolitical interests in the region).

Reagan and Bush were emboldened to act like this by the decay of the Soviet Union during the 1980s, a development that halved the number of global superpowers at a stroke. Liberated from the Cold War's logic of military escalation, Bill Clinton, in the 1990s, was sparing in the commitment overseas of US forces, other than as part of UN peacekeeping missions. Clinton was, nevertheless, attentive to other possible modalities of American dominance: global hegemony might be achieved less by naked military force than by deployment of the nation's corporate and financial power. DeLillo's *Cosmopolis*, set late in the Clinton presidency, testifies to US pre-eminence in the dizzying exchanges of money and information characteristic of this new era of globalization. However, as we show in Chapters 5 and 6, contemporary American novelists are also responsive to other dynamics of globalization, pursuing not only outward transfers of capital but also inward flows of peoples, cultures and ideas that may remodel rather than straightforwardly reproduce the United States.

The events of September 11, 2001 affirmed that, despite an abiding rhetoric of national autonomy, the US is complexly entangled in the world. Islamic militants, fighting a war as much cultural as geopolitical, flew hijacked airliners into the World Trade Center in New York, causing the deaths of 3025 people; other planes crashed fatally into the Pentagon defence headquarters in Washington, DC and, bound for a further spectacular strike on the capital city, into a Pennsylvania field. George W. Bush promptly deployed significant military force in Afghanistan to try to neuter Osama bin Laden's al-Qaeda network, responsible for the 9/11 attacks. Whereas the elder Bush was a consummate Washington insider, the younger demonstrated a populist affiliation to the vast American heartlands, sounding like the hero of a western as he promised to 'smoke out' bin Laden from his hiding-place. Bush also seemed driven by an oedipal compulsion to outdo his father when, in 2003, he launched a second Gulf War in Iraq, on thin pretexts of Saddam Hussein's complicity with 9/11 and possession of weapons of mass destruction.

As we write, however, the outcomes of Bush's 'War on Terror' are far from clear. In Iraq Saddam is dead, his dictatorship overthrown; US combat troops withdrew in the summer of 2010. American intervention has, however, left a baleful legacy, not least in countless casualties who range from the dead of high-tech aerial bombardments to inmates abused and photographed by US soldiers in Abu Ghraib prison. Meanwhile, in Afghanistan bin Laden's whereabouts are still unknown, and commentators increasingly find an analogy in the Vietnam War when assessing America's immersion in a long, attritional struggle against the Taliban. If less bloodily, a price has also been paid on US soil for this new geopolitical orientation. Only a few weeks after 9/11, Bush massively extended federal powers of surveillance and detention by rushing through Congress the USA Patriot Act (its first two words, surpassing parody, an acronym for 'Uniting and Strengthening America by Providing Appropriate Tools Required to Intercept and Obstruct Terrorism'). So far in his presidency, Obama has made changes more cosmetic than substantial to this punitive regime at home and abroad: the 'War on Terror', for example, has been rebranded as 'Overseas Contingency Operation'.

The reconfiguring of the United States as 'the Homeland Security State' (Pease 2009: 25) presents the country's novelists with new scenarios. Already, there is evidence in the post-9/11 novel of a great variety of moods and modalities: from DeLillo's elliptical narration in *Falling Man* (2007) to Jonathan Safran Foer's vivid experiments with layout and typography in *Extremely Loud and Incredibly Close* (2005), and from John Updike's attempt at imaginary, cross-racial biography in *The Terrorist* (2006) to Joseph O'Neill's postcolonial remapping of New York City in *Netherland* (2008). Despite this evidence of continuing productivity, however, literary fiction also faces, in light of the shattering events of 9/11 and afterwards, another crisis regarding its relevance and power. It is to recurrent debates about the novel's place in the contemporary US that we now turn.

CHAPTER TWO

'WHY BOTHER?': LITERARY AND INTELLECTUAL CONTEXTS OF THE CONTEMPORARY AMERICAN NOVEL

Why Bother?

Jonathan Franzen's essay 'Why Bother?', originally published in *Harper's* as 'Perchance to Dream' (1996) with the telling subtitle 'In the age of images, a reason to write novels', opens with the author admitting to his earlier 'despair about the American novel' (Franzen 2004: 55). Franzen is thinking here not of novels in general but rather of 'substantive fiction', 'serious fiction' or 'the hard stuff'. Writing of that despair in the past tense, as aligned with a period of depression from which he recovered, allows Franzen to cast at least some of his anxieties about the novel in almost comic terms, as exaggerated doubts since left behind. It also affords him a rhetorical distance from some of the essay's less fashionable critical premises. A closer reading, however, discloses that many of the factors underlying his despair are still current. The essay charts Franzen's shift from a self-conscious, inhibiting wish for the novel to matter to, and to rebuke, mainstream culture – 'to bear the weight of our whole disturbed society' (84) – to a calmer resolve to reconnect with the virtual (and, for Franzen, positively virtuous) community of readers and writers 'who read because they must' (84). Franzen is sceptical of Tom Wolfe's call in 1989 – echoing Wolfe's earlier championing of the New Journalism – for a New Social Novel that would provide 'big, rich slices of American life' (Wolfe 1989: 47). He shares with Wolfe, however, a conviction that a central merit of the novel form consists in 'its spanning of the expanse between private experience and public context' (Franzen 2004: 65). This connection between the personal and the social can help to critique, but is also threatened by, the 'atomized privacy' of US society.

For Franzen, the novel deals with permanent existential conflicts not amenable to ready solutions, 'the darkness of sorrows that have no easy cure' (79), but it does so in a surrounding 'therapeutic' culture addicted to the easy cure, that everywhere seeks to 'flatten out' such sorrows in a tyrannical, one-dimensional banality of comfortable technological consumerism. Academically speaking, this is extremely old-fashioned, and certainly unfashionable, fare, invoking clichéd and honorific notions of authenticity, with the novelist as heroic because alienated in a culture otherwise alienated from its very alienation. Although 'Why Bother?' appears always to be on the verge of revising its essentially modernist notions of literature and its relationship to the social, Franzen instead softens a felt demand for novelists to meet honorific and redemptive (if not therapeutic) aspirations that are, nevertheless, retained intact. It remains the case, for example, that the novel preserves 'substance in a time of ever-increasing evanescence' (Franzen 2004: 68). (An alternative route here might have been to argue that the novel insists on evanescence and resists attempts to disguise evanescence as substance.)

Speaking academically, though, is part of the problem for Franzen, because literature is under academic 'assault'. Novels are taught in English literature departments under the sign of a 'therapeutic optimism' resembling – rather than challenging – the shallowness of the culture at large. For Franzen, 'novels by women and cultural minorities' are taught in a reductively political fashion, as the 'darkness of these novels is not a political darkness, banishable by the enlightenment of contemporary critical theory, it's the darkness of sorrows that have no easy cure' (2004: 79). Franzen conflates politicized academic approaches to the novel with the blithe therapeutic optimism of the wider culture and opposes both to the novel's true value: namely, providing a tragic reminder of the inherent complexity and difficulty of life, raising 'more questions than it answers' and refusing to resolve 'conflict … into cant' (91).

The obvious objection to Franzen's argument is that such appeals to the tragic unhelpfully situate literature beyond the social, thereby isolating the novel from urgent processes of identity formation and cultural memory – as if political darkness weren't darkness enough. Such worries are exacerbated by Franzen's amnesiac (if eventually qualified) reflection that the tragic sense has 'tenuous purchase on the American imagination because ours is a country to which so few terrible things have ever happened' (92). More sympathetically, though, we might say that Franzen articulates the novel as a space in which the very question of what it means to be political is held vitally open, a transvaluing space offering some critical distance from the given terms of political discourse. We should also note that, in a more recent interview, Franzen modifies his position with the claim that '[s]ome of the more identity-based fiction may be more usefully and expressly instrumentalist' (Connery and Franzen 2009: 46).

The issue for Franzen, then, is less that the novel is taught in a politicized way than the specific form such politicization takes, a form that reduces complexity to the healing nostrums of an identity politics that, as he sees it, aggravates the social atomization for which it promises an easy cure. This fairly reductive rendering of identity politics overlaps with another argument that we encounter elsewhere in this book: that a progressive emphasis on difference has come at the cost of fragmentation, of producing isolated groups without a common space – literal and discursive – of cultural exchange. The African American novelist Ralph Ellison offered an early, useful expression of the sense in which the American novel aims to embody a culturally pluralist rather than multicultural vision – seeing difference as constitutive, rather than destructive, of an overarching national identity. Ellison wrote of his discovery that:

> the American novel had long concerned itself with the puzzle of the one-and-the-many; the mystery of how each of us, despite his origin in diverse regions, with our diverse racial, cultural, religious backgrounds, speaking his own diverse idiom of the American in his own accent, is, nevertheless, American. And with this concern with the implicit pluralism of the country and with the composite nature of the ideal character called "The American," there goes a concern with gauging the health of the American promise, with depicting the extent to which it was being achieved and made manifest in our daily conduct. (Ellison 1995: 207)

For Ellison, 'the small share of reality which each of our diverse groups is able to snatch from the whirling chaos of reality belongs not to the group alone, but to all of us [Americans]' (208). Franzen finds novelistic attempts to do justice to both the one and the many under threat, but is reluctant to blame novelists, identifying the problem rather with academic approaches to the novel and, oddly, television, which has 'discouraged [writers] from speaking across boundaries' because it has 'conditioned us to accept only the literal testimony of Self' (Franzen 2004: 80). He offers the following sketch of contemporary 'literary America' as resembling:

> a once-great city that had been gutted and drained by white flight and superhighways. Ringing the depressed urban core of serious fiction were prosperous new suburbs of mass entertainments. Much of the inner city's remaining vitality was concentrated in the black, Hispanic, Asian, gay and women's communities that had taken over the structures vacated by fleeing straight white males. (80)

This leaves Franzen mourning the decline of the 'broad-canvas' novel, 'a novel that's alive and multivalent like a city' (80).

Franzen is responding here to the transformation of the American literary canon reflecting the demographic and cultural transformations highlighted in Chapter 1. In the wake of the many forms of identity politics that have lately contested historical dominance in the US by older white males, the contemporary American novel has sometimes been understood less as a unified literary field than as a loose assemblage of multiple categories including women's fiction, gay and lesbian fiction, African American fiction, Native American fiction, Asian American fiction, Latino/a and Chicano/a fiction, and so on. Vital though these categories have proved in helping to redress entrenched social injustices, they have nevertheless incurred costs, not the least of which is their availability for dubious commercial exploitation. This subdividing of novelistic kinds also carries the risk of further estranging one demographic fragment of the US from another. Newer intellectual developments that include 'border theory' and the 'New American Studies' prompt considerations of the contemporary American novel less as expressions of fixed identities of an ethnic, gendered or sexual sort than as mappings of complex exchange and crossing between communities. And, as the novels to be considered in Chapters 5 and 6 indicate, such crossings may even be global or 'transnational' in scope.

It is important to note here that Franzen is considering the novel from the point of view of novelistic production – working through those ideas that turn out to be helpful, and those that turn out to be disabling, for his own novelistic practice. His essay therefore joins a long tradition of Romantic 'recovery of the will' narratives, in which necessity gives way, through an epiphany, to creative freedom. Franzen's breakthrough consists in talking down a felt demand that his novels must address, engage and rebuke 'the chimerical mainstream' (Franzen 2004: 95). This leads, however, to another aspect of Ellison's puzzle of the one and the many – that the universal, rather than forming a creative starting point, will be realized only through the particular: 'as if, in peopling and arranging my own little alternative world, I could ignore the bigger social picture even if I wanted to' (Franzen 2004: 95).

After recapturing his creativity by 'jettisoning' unhelpful obligations to engage the mainstream, Franzen went on to publish *The Corrections* (2001), which in a sense did just that. In 2001, *The Corrections* – already a bestseller – became the forty-second novel to be selected for Oprah Winfrey's phenomenally successful book club, which had begun in 1996 with an aim, as Oprah put it, 'to get the country reading again' (Travis 2007: 1017). Having become reconciled to producing 'the hard stuff' for a community of resistant readers, the selection provoked ambivalent feelings for Franzen. His reservations were several, but they included his sense that, as an author, he was 'solidly in the high-art literary tradition', whereas Oprah had selected enough 'schmaltzy, one-dimensional books' to make him 'cringe' (Kirkpatrick 2001). As rendered in the media, such comments seemed less like thoughtful ambivalence than ill-mannered elitism, leading to the cancellation of Franzen's invitation to appear on the show. Academically, too, Franzen's comments went against the cultural studies grain of exploring, rather than dismissing, 'middlebrow' cultural preferences as expressive of active and nuanced – rather than passive and unthinking – consumption. In 2009, the four bestselling hardback novels in the US were by *Twilight* author Stephenie Meyer. To dismiss such novels as pop cultural ephemera would be to foreclose the critical opportunity to assess the significance of a resurgent gothic genre that inevitably figures larger cultural concerns. Modes of 'popular' fiction are also of critical interest given their exploitability by 'literary' novels, from William Burroughs's western *The Place of Dead Roads* (1983) to Thomas Pynchon's adoption of noir in *Inherent Vice* (2009). Authors such as Walter Mosley and James

Ellroy, meanwhile, have mobilized popular formats such as crime for critical historical narratives and political explorations.

The novel as anti-product

Arguments about the health of the American novel are also – even predominantly – arguments about what we think novels are and do, clarifying and betraying the often inflated cultural values and expectations that we attribute to novels and their authors. While Franzen freed himself from exaggeratedly interventionist expectations for the novel, his subsequent argument that the novel can '*preserve* something' (Franzen 2004: 90) brings its own critical problems.

Franzen's discussion mobilizes a series of structuring and hierarchical oppositions between, for example, substance and evanescence, authentic and inauthentic, the slow work of the novel as against the hyperkinesis of the culture. In particular, Franzen differentiates the novel from technological consumerism, with the novel providing not so much a further product as an antithetical commodity:

> The consumer economy loves a product that sells at a premium, wears out quickly or is susceptible to regular improvement, and offers with each improvement some marginal gain in usefulness. To an economy like this, news that stays news is not merely an inferior product; it's an *antithetical* product. A classic work of literature is inexpensive, infinitely reusable, and, worst of all, unimprovable. (2004: 63–4)

This is an attractively minimalist instance of a larger wish for novels and their authors to constitute privileged sites that resist, and help us cognitively to map, the encroachments of technological consumerism. The wish has a long history, as Joe Moran outlines in *Star Authors*. Celebrity authors, Moran notes,

> are complex cultural signifiers who are repositories for all kinds of meanings, the most significant of which is perhaps the nostalgia for some kind of transcendent, anti-economic, creative element in a secular, debased, commercialized culture. They thus reproduce a notion, popular since the Romantic era, of authors and their work as a kind of recuperated 'other', a haven for those

creative values which an increasingly rationalistic, utilitarian society cannot otherwise accommodate. (1999: 9)

The point here is not necessarily that novels in fact lack the capacity for critique, but rather a critical awareness that the ascription of such otherwise oppositional values to novelistic production can serve to legitimize the social by advertising the continued existence of the very values that it cannot, in fact, tolerate. This places a double bind on the novelist that Franzen's essay seems to capture, with its wish to both sanctify and reconnect novelistic practice to the social. Franzen is alert to the risk, for example, of 'writing fiction that makes the same point over and over: technological consumerism is an infernal machine, technological consumerism is an infernal machine ...' (Franzen 2004: 269), and his discomfort generally resembles Norman Mailer's reflection, in 1952, that the writer's '[b]elief in the efficacy of attacking his society has been lost, but nothing has replaced the need for attack' (Mailer 1992a: 188).

If Franzen turns away from academic paradigms of identity politics in his framing of the novel's value, what is striking is the extent to which he embraces an older critical paradigm of modernism. Towards the end of 'Why Bother?', he quotes some lines from a letter of encouragement received from fellow American author Don DeLillo:

Writing is a form of personal freedom. It frees us from the mass identity we see in the making all around us. In the end, writers will write not to be outlaw heroes of some underculture but mainly to save themselves, to survive as individuals. [...] If serious reading dwindles to near nothingness, it will probably mean that the thing we're talking about when we use the word 'identity' has come to an end. (Franzen 2004: 95–6)

This sentiment can be traced back at least as far as the Frankfurt School of Marxist criticism, specifically to Adorno and Horkheimer's critique of what they termed, in the mid forties, the 'culture industry' – a phrase that, although increasingly difficult to hear as such, was intended as a contradiction in terms. Horkheimer and Adorno similarly felt that 'public life has reached a state in which thought is being turned inescapably into a commodity and language into celebration of the commodity' (2002: xiv). DeLillo's way of putting his point is telling in its apparent ambiguity. How alarmed should we be at the potential disappearance of 'the thing we're talking about when we use the word "identity"'? Might it imply, not the apocalyptic eclipse of identity as such, but rather that one way of talking about identity has given way to another? The implication here is that DeLillo aligns the novel with the preservation, not of identity as such, but with a specific and potentially limiting construction ('way of talking') about identity, and that such a way of framing literature may be even more harmful to the novel than the impinging forces of technological consumerism. As Mark Greif has shown, the notion that the novel preserves an authenticity that is under threat is nothing new; Greif considers the American critic Lionel Trilling's 1948 essay, 'Manners, Morals, and the Novel', and Trilling's sense there that, without the novel 'we shall have reason to be sad not only over a waning form of art but also over our waning freedom' (Greif 2009: 16). As Greif argues, and as indicated by DeLillo's observations, the high, culturally modernist stakes attached to the novel tend to be retained by novelists long after such approaches have become critically and academically unfashionable.

DeLillo's articulation of the novel as bound up with personal identity and resistance to technological consumerism resurfaces fairly intact in Franzen's remarks from a 2009 interview. The 'epiphanic moments' central to the novel, Franzen suggests,

> have a social and political valence as well, because they're what we mean when we talk about being a person – about being an individual, about having an identity. Identity is precisely not what consumer culture says it is. It's not the playlist on your iPod. It's not your personal preference in denim washes. The moment you become an individual is the moment when all that consumer stuff falls away and you're left with the narrativity of your own life. All the things that would become impossible – politically, emotionally, culturally, psychologically – if people ever were to become simply the sum of their consumer choices: this is, indirectly, what the novel is trying to preserve and fight in favour of. (Connery and Franzen 2009: 36)

The issue here is less one of connecting the social and the personal than one of preserving intact a threatened subjectivity, of refusing the wrong kind of intrusion of the public into the private. This association of the novel with subjectivity, or with 'what might formerly have been called the soul, and what I might now describe as some interior locus of privacy and reflection where moments of personal significance are experienced' (Connery and Franzen 2009: 36), leads Franzen to a sharp, if questionable, contrast between the novel and technology. For Franzen, '[a]s great as our various glowing screens may be at capturing vividness and complexity, you're still always on the outside just looking at them. You're never within' (Connery and Franzen 2009: 36).

The reader is also, of course, always 'on the outside' of – at arm's length from – the book, so Franzen's opposition here between the page and the screen testifies primarily to his prior, ideological wish to construct the novel in terms of interiority. We will further challenge and explore this either/or – page *versus* screen – in Chapter 7, where we consider the various afterlives which contemporary American novels have in film adaptations, videogames and internet fan clubs. Philip Roth has invoked a similarly sharp opposition between the novel and technology. In *The Human Stain* (2000), for example, discussed in Chapter 4, the narrator intends his novel to counter 'scurrilous' distortions proliferated by an anonymous online discussion posting; the implied hope is that his novel might mitigate the outbreak of a cultural 'epidemic' of stupidity: 'It was there. The pathogens were out there. In the ether. In the universal hard drive, everlasting and undeletable' (Roth 2001: 291). In an interview from 2000, Roth further opposes the page and the screen:

> The evidence is everywhere that the literary era has come to an end [...] The evidence is the culture, the evidence is the society, the evidence is the screen, the progression from the movie screen to the television screen to the computer. There's only so much time, so much room, and there are only so many habits of mind that can determine how people use the free time they have. Literature takes a habit of mind that has disappeared. It requires silence, some form of isolation, and sustained concentration in the presence of an enigmatic thing. (Remnick 2007: 119)

Roth connects the end of 'the literary era' to the waning of the modernist preoccupation with the exploration of consciousness, and its attendant hermeneutic of looking beneath the surface: 'It's no longer of interest. I think that what we're seeing is the narrowing of consciousness. [...] The writer is just not of interest to the public as somebody who may have an inroad into consciousness' (Remnick 2007: 119). As pessimistic (and as familiar) as this sounds, Roth portrays the 'death of reading' in slightly less apocalyptic terms than DeLillo by describing it as continuous, not with the eclipse of identity as such, but with a wider process in which 'the American branch of the species is being retooled' (Remnick 2007: 120).

Updating the universal hard drive

As our case studies of a diverse range of novels in Chapters 3 to 6 demonstrate, the contemporary American novel remains actively implicated in the processes governing the fashioning and refashioning of US national identity. Far from being shackled to backward-looking and preservationist projects, it is comprehensively entangled in 'new ways of talking' about personal and national identity, or updating 'the universal hard drive'. In Chapter 3, we consider Bret Easton Ellis's *American Psycho* (1991) and Chuck Palahniuk's *Fight Club* (1996) as twin explorations of the systemic violence of consumer capitalism. Unearthing the serial violence of serial consumerism, both novels are shown to provoke urgent questions about the form that critique might take within a capitalist system adept at repackaging dissent as a further, compelling commodity suffused with a glamorous aura of subversion. Although valuing postmodern approaches that usefully complicate easy oppositions between 'pure' and 'impure' critique, we nevertheless find that the postmodern horizon of consumption, rather than production, works to sustain a premature sense of the futility of critique. Chapter 4 juxtaposes Toni Morrison's *Beloved* (1987) and Roth's *The Human Stain* (2000), two very different narratives of identity that, together, complicate recent understandings of the US as having entered a post-racial epoch, suggesting instead a nation still haunted by slavery and racial divisions. If Morrison's revisionist, historio-graphical novel draws on identity politics to memorialize and give voice to the 'Sixty Million or More' lost to slavery's Middle Passage, Roth's novel confronts the potentially essentialist logic of identity politics with the 'sliding relationship with everything' (Roth 2001: 108) sought by its main protagonist.

In Chapter 5, Cormac McCarthy's *Blood Meridian* (1985), Leslie Marmon Silko's *Almanac of the Dead* (1991) and Junot Díaz's *The*

Brief Wondrous Life of Oscar Wao (2007) are seen to underscore the importance of undertaking a conceptual shift from nation to hemisphere, thinking not of the 'American' but of the 'Americas' novel, thereby resisting the imperialist conflation of 'American' with the culture of the United States. The expansive, transnational conception of 'American' that these novels invoke entails a critical remapping that resists, but also risks attesting to, the continued power of US imperialism. In Chapter 6, we trace the workings of transnational capital in Bharati Mukherjee's *Jasmine* (1989) and Don DeLillo's *Cosmopolis* (2003), texts exploring the rhetoric and reality of increasingly prominent discourses of globalization. We find that both novels not only represent but also critically engage with the complex and contradictory currents of globalization, mapping both its violent homogenization and its creative heterogenization.

A central argument of this book, therefore, is that the contemporary American novel – despite prominent, premature laments over its supersession – constitutes a dynamic, politically and culturally engaged form, thoroughly entangled with, and staging critical interventions into, the social, cultural and political forces shaping US identity at both the national and transnational levels. Franzen, meanwhile, having decried the lack of novelists on the cover of *Time* magazine as indicative of a broader cultural neglect, found himself on the cover in August of 2010, alongside the banner 'Great American Novelist', to publicize his latest novel, *Freedom* (2010). It was also reported that President Barack Obama had packed *Freedom* among his summer vacation reading, having perhaps joined Franzen's virtual community of resistant readers.

REVIEW, READING AND RESEARCH

Chapter 1: 'Who Are We?'

Review

- The rise and dramatic fall of the US economy from 1980 to the present is an inescapable influence on, and topic for, contemporary American fiction.
- The US has been deeply divided during the period covered in this book by the 'culture wars': highly charged debates between conservatives and progressives over American cultural values and national identity.
- Significant demographic shifts in the US have led conservatives to voice anxieties about cultural and linguistic diversity and the erosion of a 'core' culture, anxieties that liberals and radicals interpret as nostalgia for ethnic privilege.
- The legacy of George W. Bush's 'War on Terror', declared after the 9/11 attacks on the US, is uncertain, with Iraq currently in flux and commentators drawing parallels between America's fight against the Taliban in Afghanistan and the Vietnam War.

Reading

Dawson, A. and Schueller, M. J. (2007), 'Introduction: rethinking imperialism today', in A. Dawson and M. J. Schueller (eds), *Exceptional State: Contemporary US Culture and the New Imperialism*. Durham, NC: Duke University Press, pp. 1–33.

Duncan, R. and Goddard, J. (2009), *Contemporary America* (3rd edn). Basingstoke: Palgrave Macmillan.

Grosfoguel, R., Maldonado-Torres, N. and Saldívar, J. D. (2005), 'Latin@s and the "Euro-American menace": the decolonization of the US empire in the twenty-first century', in R. Grosfoguel, N. Maldonado-Torres and J. D. Saldívar (eds), *Latin@s in the World-System: Decolonization Struggles in the Twenty-First Century US Empire*. Boulder, CO: Paradigm, pp. 3–27.

Huntington, S. (2004), *Who Are We?: America's Great Debate*. London: Free Press.

Pease, D. E. (2009), *The New American Exceptionalism*. Minneapolis: University of Minnesota Press.

Wallerstein, I. (2003), *The Decline of American Power: The US in a Chaotic World*. New York: The New Press.

Research

- Identify some of the key fantasies and phobias regarding national identity explored by contemporary American fiction from 1980 to the present.
- Where can we find examples, in contemporary American fiction, of excavations and re-presentations of the past that exert an influence on the present? You might, for instance, track African American remembrances of slavery across not only the fiction of Toni Morrison (discussed below in Chapter 4) but across such novels as David Bradley's *The Chaneysville Incident* (1981), Sherley Anne Williams's *Dessa Rose* (1986) and Phyllis Alesia Perry's *Stigmata* (1998).
- What similarities and differences can you find among American novels that take 9/11 as their subject matter? To what extent and to what effect do these novels deploy formal experimentation in order to represent terrorism and its aftermath?

Chapter 2: 'Why Bother?'

Review

- Many writers feel uncertain about the status and role of the novel in the advanced media landscape of the contemporary US.
- The novel has been a vital and dynamic resource in the debates surrounding identity politics, in felt tension with the notion that the American novel should represent the nation as a whole.
- The apparent contrast between the novel and newer forms of technology – from television to the web – has been aggravated and exaggerated by dated and defensive notions of the novel form.

Reading

Connery, C. and Franzen, J. (2009), 'The liberal form: an interview with Jonathan Franzen'. *boundary 2* 36, 2: 31–54.

Ellison, R. (1995), 'Hidden name and complex fate', in J. F. Callahan (ed.), *The Collected Essays of Ralph Ellison*. New York: Random House/The Modern Library, pp. 189–209.

Franzen, J. (2004), 'Why bother?', in *How to be Alone: essays*. London: Harper Perennial.

Greif, M. (2009), '"The death of the novel" and its afterlives: toward a history of the "big, ambitious novel."' *boundary 2* 36, 2: 11–30.

Horkheimer, M. and Adorno, T. W. (2002), 'The culture industry: enlightenment as mass deception', in G. S. Noerr (trans.) and E. Jephcott (ed.), *Dialectic of Enlightenment: Philosophical Fragments*. Stanford: Stanford University Press, pp. 95–136.

Kirkpatrick, D. D. (2001), 'Winfrey rescinds offer to author for guest appearance.' *New York Times*. October 24.

Mailer, N. (1992a), 'Our country and our culture. Contribution to *Partisan Review* symposium', in *Advertisements for Myself*. Cambridge, MA: Harvard University Press.

Moran, J. (1999), *Star Authors: Literary Celebrity in America*. London: Pluto.

Remnick, D. (2007), 'Into the clear: Philip Roth', in *Reporting*. London: Picador, pp. 101–24.

Wolfe, T. (1989), 'Stalking the billion-footed beast: a literary manifesto for the new social novel'. *Harper's*. November, 45–56.

—(1996), 'The new journalism', in E. W. Johnson and T. Wolfe (eds), *The New Journalism*. New York: Harper and Row, pp. 15–68.

Research

- Do you agree that the novel form is in some sense an 'anti-commodity'?
- What are the strengths and weaknesses of the critical assumption that the American novel must somehow represent the nation as a whole?
- How can we challenge the assumption that the novel lacks a foothold in a kinetic society dominated by technological consumerism, without reverting to dated and defensive ideas of literature?

PART TWO

TEXTS

CHAPTER THREE

OVERPOWERING CONSUMERISM

AMERICAN PSYCHO (1991) AND *FIGHT CLUB* (1996)

'You are not a beautiful and unique snowflake'

Mary Gaitskill's short story 'The Dentist' (1997) opens with an image of a woman obsessed with an image of a woman advertising Obsession:

> In Jill's neighbourhood there was a giant billboard advertisement for a perfume called Obsession. It was mounted over the chain grocery store at which she shopped [...] It was a close-up black-and-white photograph of an exquisite girl with the fingers of one hand pressed against her open lips. Her eyes were fixated, wounded, deprived. At the same time, her eyes were flat. Her body was slender, almost starved, giving her delicate beauty the strange, arrested sensuality of unsatisfied want. But her fleshy lips and enormous eyes were sumptuously, even grossly abundant. The photograph loomed over the toiling shoppers like a totem of sexualized pathology [...] At least this is what Jill thought about it, but Jill was an essayist who wrote primarily for magazines, and she was prone to extravagant mental tangents based on very little. (1998: 137)

This provocative tableau displays key features from the everyday landscape of consumer society: the pervasive presence and potency of advertising; the cultural obsession with bodies, models and images; and the economics of fantasy, fetishism and sadomasochistic desire. At the same time, Gaitskill offers her reader a reminder about the possibility of over-reading the signs of consumer culture. It is, of course, important to be wary of 'extravagant mental tangents based on very little', but the pitfalls of over-reading consumerism must be weighed against the danger of succumbing to analytical anorexia and a critical silence implicit in the image above of 'almost starved' fingers 'pressed against [...] open lips'.

Any discussion of contemporary American fiction has to talk about consumerism. Arguably, consumerism constitutes *the* essential context for understanding contemporary literature and society. Between 1950 and 1997, the year in which 'The Dentist' was published, the 'global consumption of goods and services [...] multiplied by a factor of six' (Bauman 2001: 114). A sizable portion of this increase took place in America. The US makes up approximately five percent of the world population, but is responsible for around forty percent of global consumption. According to Benjamin Barber, consumerism in America is:

> *ubiquitous* (it is everywhere); it is *omnipresent* (it is 'all the time' and aspires to fill up all time); it is *addictive* (it creates its own forms of reinforcement); it is *self-replicating* (it spreads virally); and is *omnilegitimate* (it engages in active self-rationalization and self-justification, eroding the moral bases for resisting it). (2007: 222)

We should note that Jill's encounter above with consumerism does not take place inside the 'chain grocery store' but on the street outside. The supermarket and the mall are crucial sites for capitalism, but Barber reminds us that consumerism can also be found 'on sidewalks and walls and buses and trains, in school-rooms and bedrooms and restrooms and trams, on big screens and pod-screens and TVs and phones, carved into haircuts and written on skin' (224).

Consumerism increasingly penetrates all areas of contemporary American society and this expansion is reflected in contemporary American fiction. Consumerism is at the core of the novels we will be considering in this chapter – *American Psycho* (1991) and *Fight Club* (1996) – as well as other fiction by their authors. Elsewhere on the literary scene representations differ wildly – from, say, retail therapy for a 'must-have' pair of Manolo Blahnik sling-backs in Candace Bushnell's *Sex and the City* (1997) to the surreal appearance of a Coke can and a shopping trolley in Cormac

McCarthy's post-apocalyptic *The Road* (2006) – but the inescapable fact of consumerism itself looms large in recent fiction. It should not be assumed that this is a new phenomenon. American fiction has engaged with consumerism since its origins and in fact one might detect an allusion by Gaitskill to one of the seminal literary engagements with this subject: F. Scott Fitzgerald's *The Great Gatsby* (1925). With his mansion, lavish parties, a yellow Rolls Royce and a wardrobe crammed with silk shirts, Fitzgerald's eponymous hero is the lyric poet of a burgeoning consumer society in Jazz Age America. Whilst Gatsby offers the reader one face for consumerism, a second, more ominous avatar features in a billboard advertisement in the midst of an ashen wasteland:

> But above the gray land and the spasms of bleak dust which drift endlessly over it, you perceive, after a moment, the eyes of Doctor T. J. Eckleburg. The eyes of Doctor T. J. Eckleburg are blue and gigantic – their retinas are one yard high. (Fitzgerald 1990: 86)

As Jill focuses on the eyes of a model on a billboard, the reader might see a second pair belonging to the oculist from *The Great Gatsby*. Both Gaitskill's and Fitzgerald's personifications of the ever-watchful gods of consumerism might in turn be framed by the Marxist theoretician Walter Benjamin's description, in the 1920s, of advertising imagery as a 'phantasmagoria', or collective fantasy realm, where we encounter 'the face of the huge images spread across the walls of houses, where toothpaste and cosmetics lie handy for giants' (2004: 476).

In the 1920s the advertising industry (which employed Fitzgerald for a brief period) played a vital role in the birth of the first fully-fledged consumer society. Advertising encouraged consumers to purchase, often on credit, a range of new products that included automobiles, washing machines, refrigerators, vacuum cleaners and toasters. In 1925, the year that *The Great Gatsby* was published, spending on advertising in the US reached a record high of approximately $2.6 billion. By 1997, the year that Gaitskill's 'The Dentist' appeared, this figure had risen to around $200 billion (Klein 2001: 11). In *Generation X* (1991), Douglas Coupland cites the following corroboratory statistics: 'the [n]umber of commercials American children see by age 18: 350,000. The foregoing amount expressed

in days (based on an average of 40 seconds per commercial): 160'
(1996: 210). Over and above the promotion of a particular product,
the primary function of advertising is to inculcate the act of
consumption itself: to encourage the consumer to equate happiness
with the acquisition of certain commodities. In isolation, Jill's
response to the advert for Obsession might seem disproportionate,
but it needs to be viewed within the context of a society in which
ambient advertising is virtually inescapable. Christopher Lasch
proposes that universal consumerism and advertising combine to
'create a world of mirrors, insubstantial images, illusions increasingly indistinguishable from reality' (1985: 30). The image is a mirror
in which the consumer sees her own lack: the absence of a particular
product, a type of body, a person she is not but might yet be.

A second mirroring worth noting at this juncture involves a
blurring of the lines between advertising and art. As writers and
other artists have increasingly turned their attention towards
consumerism, consumerism itself, as is evident in the carefully
crafted portraiture for Obsession, has made ever more extensive use
of aesthetics. Advertising, what we might call the 'official' art form
of capitalism, is increasingly abstract and self-referential. In this
regard, we should note a significant omission from Jill's detailed
description of the advertisement for a perfume: the product itself
is missing from a minimalist *mise-en-scène* which features only
a model and a brand name. Calvin Klein was a prominent and
commercially successful brand during the 80s and 90s. The success
of this corporation was largely attributable to a controversial use of
sexual imagery in its marketing and the prioritization of the brand
itself over the product: replicating the strategy that marketed boxer
shorts and jeans as 'Calvins', the fragrance is advertised as Calvin
Klein's *Obsession*. In *No Logo*, Naomi Klein (no relation) offers
a strident critique of visual and auditory pollution by corporate
brands. She contends that Calvin Klein, alongside corporations
such as Tommy Hilfiger, Nike and Pepsi, were at the forefront of
a crucial development in contemporary consumer capitalism: what
these organizations 'produced primarily were not things, they said,
but "images" of their brands. Their real work lay not in manufacturing but in marketing' (Klein 2001: 4). Instead of using a logo to
sell a product, Klein contends that corporations began to see the
product itself as a tool with which to maintain and develop their
brand identity. On the 'brandscape' of advanced consumer society,

the commodity is eclipsed by the logo, the image, the sign. What a product does is increasingly secondary to what it is called, how it is advertised, consumed and displayed as a signifier of a certain style or fashion. Although the casual assumption might be made that a consumer society is profoundly materialistic, it is also, to return to Benjamin's term, a 'phantasmagoria': a realm in which the concrete commodity is displaced by diaphanous dreams and desires.

It would be problematic, however, to assume that everything in the consumer society has melted into a phantasmagoria of promissory images. Despite the dematerializing forces around it, the body retains a potent materiality. According to Jean Baudrillard, 'in the consumer package, there is one object finer, more precious and more dazzling than any other [...] That object is the BODY' (1998: 129). A key function of advertising is to promote concerns about the messy materialism of the consumer's body. Jill's encounter with the advert for Obsession might be read as an exemplary moment for a society in which consumers are continually assailed by images of practically unobtainable 'perfection'. Advertising appears to promote positive images, but its covert imperative is to encourage obsessive anxiety about our bodies: how they look, feel and smell; what enters, comes out of and goes over them. Consumers are besieged by body images which aim to persuade them that they are deficient in some way. Typically, the body is fragmented into 'problem areas' that require permanent regulation and maintenance with regard to every aspect of shape and size, diet and adornment. The gaze of the model is so pervasive that it is internalized and the consumer accordingly subjects him- or herself to a disciplinary self-surveillance.

The enormous 'wounded' eyes and 'almost starved' body of the model advertising Obsession exemplify the sexual imagery routinely deployed by advertisers and hint at sadomasochistic undercurrents beneath the squeaky clean surfaces of contemporary body culture. As long ago as 1959, the novelist Norman Mailer asserted that '[s]ex has become the centre of our economy' (1992b: 431). Mailer's provocative contention is confirmed by the success of Calvin Klein who initially rose to prominence in 1980 with a campaign promoting jeans that used a fifteen-year old actress, Brooke Shields, and the slogan 'nothing comes between me and my Calvins'. The corporation's subsequent use of semi-naked teenage models for billboard ads in the 90s led to allegations of child pornography and investigations by the FBI. 'Sex sells' and strains of masochistic desire might even be detected in the everyday routines and rituals inflicted on the consumer body: the denials of dieting and socially-sanctioned 'torture' of gym regimes; waxing and colonic irrigation; tattooing and body piercing; Botox and collagen implants; liposuction, limb lengthening and 'tummy tuck'; facelifts and chemical peels; breast implants, designer vaginas and penis enlargements.

The promotion of self-surveillance and modes of masochistic self-torture in accordance with ideals of 'beauty' and fashion has traditionally been directed towards women. Since the 1980s, however, there has been a dramatic rise in the targeting of male consumers. In this chapter we will trace tangents (hopefully not too 'extravagant') from the opening page of 'The Dentist' through two novels by male authors. We will examine Ellis's and Palahniuk's representation in *American Psycho* and *Fight Club* of the hazy lines between bodies and commodities, sex and violence, advertising and pornography, models and mirrors in the phantasmagorical visual culture of consumerism. We will conclude by looking briefly at a final problematic fuzziness which is evident as the critique of commodification threatens to elide with the commodification of critique.

AMERICAN PSYCHO: SUPERMARKET DE SADE

At one point in *American Psycho* the eponymous protagonist, Patrick Bateman, masturbates while thinking about 'a near-naked model in a halter top I saw today in a Calvin Klein advertisement' (Ellis 1997: 23). In addition to fashion photography, Bateman is also stimulated by television and film. He rents Brian De Palma's *Body Double* (1984) thirty-seven times 'to masturbate over the scene where the woman is getting drilled to death by a power-drill' (67). Bateman's obsessive onanism might be seen both as a sign and symptom of the 'pornification' of popular culture (Paasonen 2007). In addition to its development as a multi-billion dollar global industry, pornography has become an integral feature of mainstream consumer society: softcore imagery is now routinely deployed in advertising, music video, television, film and on the internet. Bateman's masturbatory practices testify to the pervasiveness of pornography and point towards the main target in Ellis's seriocomic critique of consumerism: the sexualization of commodities and violence in fantasy images of bodies, fashions and models that encourage addiction, seriality and uncanny doublings.

The most uncanny doubling in *American Psycho* is that which twins the serial killer with the consumer. Patrick Bateman does two things: he consumes and he kills with the same steroid-infused intensity. The novel is stuffed with exhaustive catalogues of Bateman's possessions: a luxury apartment with ultra-fashionable furnishings, designer clothes and beauty products, CDs and music equipment, video players and camcorders, and innumerable luxury purchases at restaurants, gyms, health spas, concerts and clubs. These interminable shopping lists are juxtaposed with an equally excessive inventory of rape, torture and serial murder. Transgressive violence and extravagant consumption are not merely counter-pointed, but frequently conjoined as, for example, when Bateman considers 'killing someone with an Allsop Racer ski pole' (Ellis 1997: 281). *American Psycho* is founded, then, on an audacious and alarming analogy between conspicuous consumption and serial murder. As James Annesley notes, in '*American Psycho* the word "consume" is used in all of its possible meanings: purchasing, eating and destroying' (1998: 16). Is Ellis's novel founded on anything more substantial than a lexical coincidence, or might there be a critical connection between Bateman's different types of 'consumption'? To answer this question we need to consider the multiple meanings of a second key term: *violence*. In this context, Slavoj Žižek has argued that 'we should learn to step back, to disentangle ourselves from the fascinating lure of this distinctly visible "subjective" violence, violence performed by a clearly identifiable agent. We need to perceive the contours of the background which generates such outbursts' (2008: 1). Žižek proposes a structural link between forms of highly visible 'subjective' violence – 'acts of crime and terror' reported in the media – and a largely invisible but pervasive 'systemic' violence inherent to the 'normal, peaceful state of things' (1–2). *American Psycho* aims to present precisely this link between the 'subjective' violence of Patrick Bateman and the 'systemic' violence of consumer capitalism.

One of the most conspicuous clichés in the discourses of serial killing concerns the terrifying normality of the murderer: his violence is concealed beneath a facade of unthreatening ordinariness. Critics of consumerism would propose that the system's inherent violence is similarly ciphered beneath a veneer of 'choice', 'pleasure' and 'style'. Throughout its history, consumer capitalism has been under-pinned by an infrastructure of violence. In the nineteenth century an emerging consumer system was entangled in slavery and colonial expansion (in Chapters 4 and 5 we will see graphic examples of this in *Beloved* and *Blood Meridian*). In the twentieth century, consumer booms in the 1920s and 1950s were contingent on increased industrial capacity achieved during the First and Second World Wars. Conflicts in the Persian Gulf during the late twentieth and early twenty-first centuries have been driven by the need to guarantee access to the oil which fuels car cultures. The green lobby seeks to highlight the devastating environmental violence of consumerism: climate change, waste and pollution as well as the systematic torture and slaughter of other species for food, clothing and medicine. The bodies of workers, including millions of children, in factories and sweatshops in the developing world are subjected to the violence of routine exploitation and industrial accidents to produce commodities for consumption in the overdeveloped world. Consumer capitalism generates radical inequalities on the global level and within nations that result in violent conflict, crime, trauma and psychological stress.

American Psycho is set in a milieu – Reagan's America – that, as was mentioned in Chapter 1, witnessed massive increases in both consumption and inequality. Reaganomics reduced taxes and interest rates to stimulate consumer spending. Increased levels of affluence among the baby boomers (the generation born after the Second World War) and a concurrent willingness to take on unprecedented levels of debt (mortgages, loans, credit cards) resulted in a property boom as well as record sales of luxury cars, designer clothing and new gadgets such as VCRs and home computers, microwave ovens and food processors, cordless phones and answering machines. Ostentatious displays of wealth were *de rigueur* among young urban professionals (Yuppies), and the zeitgeist of rampant materialism was evident throughout popular culture: from Madonna's 'Material Girl' (1985) and the media infatuation with tycoon celebrities (such as Donald Trump and Michael Milken) to Gordon Gekko's infamous catchphrase in Oliver Stone's *Wall Street* (1987): 'greed is good'. The economic policies which promoted unbridled consumerism widened the gap between rich and poor and increased poverty and homelessness. The Janus-faced features of the Reagan 80s are reflected throughout *American Psycho*. Ellis's *über*-yuppie embodies the era's excesses with his unchecked conspicuous consumption of status symbols: Bateman is obsessed with executive cars, *haute couture* and technological toys. He slides slickly between exclusive restaurants and gyms, penthouse apartments and the air-conditioned offices of Wall Street, but then also roams the run-down areas of the city in search of victims. Bateman's targets include those who have already been already targeted by the dominant culture – his vicious attacks on the homeless can be read not as an exception to, but rather an extension of, the 'normal, peaceful state of things'. Bateman's rabid ultra-violence against all those marginalized by the New Right in the US in the 1980s – the destitute and the working class, racial and ethnic minorities, women, bohemians and queers – positions *American Psycho* as the unconscious of Reagan's America.

American Psycho relentlessly equates compulsory consumerism with compulsive violence. When Bateman describes the sensation of his first act of violence – an attack on a homeless African American in a back alley – he relies on consumer tropes:

> I feel ravenous, pumped up, as if I'd just worked out [...] or just embraced the first line of cocaine, inhaled the first puff of a fine cigar, sipped the first glass of Cristal. I'm starving and need something to eat. (Ellis 1997: 132)

As we consume its images of barbarism, *American Psycho* invites the reader to consider monstrous violence as a gothic mirroring of the everyday violence concealed within consumer capitalism. Bateman's assault on the bodies of others can be read both as a grotesque extension of the violence inflicted on the marginalized and of the discipline which consumers are trained to impose on their own bodies:

> I worked out heavily at the gym after leaving the office today but the tension has returned, so I do ninety abdominal crunches, a hundred and fifty push-ups, and then I run in place for twenty minutes whilst listening to the new Huey Lewis and the News CD. I take a hot shower and afterwards use a new facial scrub. (76)

The 80s witnessed a health and fitness craze alongside a massive increase in sales of cosmetics for men. In his daily exercise and beauty regime, Bateman evinces the consumer society's narcissistic obsession with a model body which is disturbingly close to a mannequin: 'my stomach is as taut as possible, my chest steel, pectorals granite hard, my eyes white as ice' (370). In his pioneering exploration of the birth of modern consumerism in the Parisian Arcades of the nineteenth century, Walter Benjamin noted that the fashion mannequin was 'the model for imitation' (1999: 78). The mannequin also epitomizes the ideal of 80s body culture: tall, youthful, slim, impervious to wrinkles and blemishes, illness and aging. Bateman's obsession with the designer clothing worn by those in his social circle underlines their status as ambulatory shop window dummies. His fetishistic fascination with 'hard bodies' – both the muscular torso built in the gym and the stiff and frozen body parts he collects – similarly attests to the charismatic cult of the mannequin. The logical next step in the process of self-objectification is to treat the bodies of other people as objects. Bateman's masochistic punishment of his own body in the gym is complemented by his sadistic assaults on others. What the monstrous serial killer does to the bodies of his victims might also be read as a gothic metaphor for what normally happens to the body in the media and advertising: Bateman's dismemberment of the human form queerly reflects the visual culture of a consumer society in which the body is remorselessly cut-up and recycled as images of isolated parts ('perfect' hair and teeth, 'perfect' stomach and chest).

Bateman not only disassembles but also eats the bodies of his victims: he chews skin from fingers, devours a brain, bakes femurs and jawbones and fries a breast. Although this gothic gorging constitutes a shocking transgression of cultural taboo, Ellis also characterizes the serial killer's necrophagy, once again, not as a deviation so much as a hyperbolic amplification of everyday consumer desires. *American Psycho* opens in a restaurant on the first of April with a feast of fools and is subsequently glutted with an endless round of dinner and lunch dates as well as constant references to food and drink. In the final stages of his rampage, Bateman begins to hint at explicit analogies between this excessive consumption and his obscene cannibalism: 'Her stomach resembles the eggplant and goat cheese lasagne at Il Marlibro or some other kind of dog food' (Ellis 1997: 344); and 'I buy a Dove Bar, a coconut one, in which I find part of a bone' (386). Consumerism, needless to say, does not literally condone cannibalism, but a figurative analogy might be drawn between classical anthropophagic practices and contemporary capitalist excesses: the rapacious consumption of land, labour and resources in acts of destructive wastefulness. In Patrick Bateman, primitive energies erupt through the civilized mask of the yuppie consumer to expose what Deborah Root has called the 'cannibal unconscious' of late capitalism (1996: 3).

Driven by a primitive orality, Bateman is fundamentally unable to differentiate between people and things: everyone and everything he encounters is perceived as a series of consumables that exist solely for his pleasure. According to its critics, consumerism produces 'reification': put simply, the tendency to treat people as objects and objects as people. The collection of fetish objects is part of the M.O. of the serial killer and is evident in *American Psycho*:

> things are lying in the corner of my bedroom: a pair of girl's shoes from Edward Susan Bennis Allen, a hand with the thumb and fore-finger missing, the new issue of *Vanity Fair* splashed with someone's blood, a cummerbund drenched with gore. (Ellis 1997: 343–4)

Bateman cannot distinguish between these objects but is simply driven by the lust to consume them. His compulsive collection of objects appears compensatory for his lack of meaningful relations with other people. As Jean Baudrillard suggests, the object is never merely itself but always 'at the same time *an indication of the absence of a human relationship*' (2005: 193). In Baudrillard's bleak prognosis the 'luxuriant growth of objects [...] an ever-accelerating procession of generations of products, appliances and gadgets' (2005: 3) signifies the implosion of social relations into commodity fetishism: 'everything now conspires to make objects into the fodder of relationships, and relationships themselves (whether sexual, marital, familial or microsocial) into a mere framework for the consumption of objects' (2005: 69).

In a chapter entitled 'Shopping', Bateman itemizes *ad nauseam* the objects he intends to purchase as Christmas presents: 'pens and photo albums, pairs of bookends and light-weight luggage, electric shoe polishers and heated towel stands and silver-plated insulated carafes and portable palm-sized color TVs with earphones, birdhouses and candleholders, place mats, picnic hampers and ice buckets (Ellis 1997: 177). Indefatigable cataloguing of objects is conspicuous throughout *American Psycho* as Ellis mimics the stylistics of the shopping list or catalogue. Different brands of consumption – from Christmas shopping to renting porn and eating internal organs – are all described in the same flat, affectless tone. The android atonality of Ellis's 'blank fiction' underscores the fact that Bateman gets little pleasure and certainly no lasting sense of fulfillment from the objects he consumes. In fact, he finds himself trapped in a vicious circle of affluence: the more objects he acquires the more he becomes dependent upon them. To return to Baudrillard, the consumer society operates according to the 'logic of desire' and desire does not stop:

> And just one object no longer suffices: the fulfilment of the project of possession always means a succession or even a complete series of objects. This is why owning absolutely any object is always so satisfying and so disappointing at the same time: a whole series lies behind any single object, and makes it into a source of anxiety. (2005: 86)

Bateman's consumerism is inexorably serial. He consumes serial forms of mass culture: in between repeat viewings of *Body Double*, he watches daily reruns of *The Patty Winters Show* and video footage of plane crashes, he reads reviews and fashion tips in weekly magazines and looks out for crime stories in the newspapers and on TV. On a shopping expedition, Bateman finds himself mesmerized by 'the rows, the endless rows of ties' (Ellis 1997: 296). Bateman collects clothes in series (matching suits, shirts and shoes), beauty products, music CDs, multiple varieties of mineral water, recipes and menus. Alongside this catalogue of serial objects and spectacles, *American Psycho* depicts a range of serial spaces (identical and inter-changeable office buildings, restaurants, nightclubs and apartment buildings which Bateman continually confuses) and serial selves (all of Bateman's yuppie friends are continually mistaken for each other). Despite advertising's promise of the 'unique' and 'individual' there are no *singular* but only *serial* objects in consumer society. In this context, Mark Seltzer has proposed that:

> the question of serial killing cannot be separated from the general forms of seriality, collection and counting conspicuous in consumer society [...] and the forms of fetishism – the collecting of things and representations, persons and person-things like bodies – that traverse it. (1998: 64)

Bateman collects and counts with a fetishistic intensity. Each time he recites the details of his exercise regimen the number of repetitions increases. The incessant repetition of repetition in the text underscores the addictive nature of Bateman's behaviour and might prompt the question: at what point does compulsory consumerism become compulsive?

Bateman's clearly compulsive consumerism cannot be reduced to the simple possession of serial objects since it also involves the magical aura of specific brands. James Annesley reminds us that Ellis's characters 'don't drive cars, they drive "BMWs", they don't eat in restaurants, they eat in "Spago's", they don't wear sunglasses, they wear "Raybans"' (1998: 7). The reader of *American Psycho* is buffeted by a blizzard of brands which white out the products to which they are attached. The absurdity of Bateman's brand loyalty is foregrounded by his obsession with bottled waters whose only significant difference is their label. In consumer society the function and 'use-value' of a commodity is often secondary to style or what Baudrillard terms 'sign-value': '*to become an object of consumption, an object must first become a sign*' (Baudrillard 2005: 200). Bateman is a connoisseur of sign-value and automatically identifies logos and labels: 'Evelyn's wearing a cotton blouse by Dolce & Gabbana, suede shoes by Yves Saint Laurent, a stencilled calf shirt by Adrienne Landau with a suede belt by Jill Stuart, Calvin Klein tights, Venetian-glass earrings by Frances Patiky Stein' (Ellis 1997: 20). The brand-name overkill in *American Psycho* becomes a product placement *for* product placement: the foregrounding of a cultural and economic practice which threatens to become less visible as it becomes more pervasive.

In a dismissive review of *American Psycho* entitled 'Snuff This Book! Will Bret Easton Ellis Get away with Murder?', Roger Rosenblatt attributes the obsession with brands not to Bateman but the author:

> I do not exaggerate when I say that in his way Mr. Ellis may be the most knowledgeable author in all of American literature. Whatever Melville knew about whaling, whatever Mark Twain knew about rivers are mere amateur stammering compared with what Mr. Ellis knows about shampoo alone. (1990)

We might detect a jibe about the author's machismo in Rosenblatt's contrast between muscular nautical labours and the effeminate consumer obsessed with beauty products. A less catty and more pertinent literary kinship might be suggested between Ellis and F. Scott Fitzgerald. In his essay, 'The Crack-Up' (1936), Fitzgerald described the 1920s as 'an age of excess [...] [a] whole race going hedonistic, deciding on pleasure' (Fitzgerald 2009: 15). In this regard, the Jazz Age can be twinned with the Reagan 80s as eras of rampant consumerism. Karl Marx, echoing Hegel, famously claimed that historical figures and events appear twice: 'the first time as tragedy, the second time as farce' (Marx 1993: 287). In the fiction of Fitzgerald and Ellis we see history repeating itself but with the lyrical modernist tragedy of Gatsby replaced by the grotesque farce and postmodern pastiche of Patrick Bateman. Although both characters rely on commodities to define their identities, Gatsby sees them as a means to an end: 'enchanted objects' (Fitzgerald 1990: 98) designed to win the heart of Daisy Buchanan. Bateman, however, is a gothic Gatsby with no love object other than himself. The romantic tragic hero is replaced by a farcical narcissistic monster.

Despite this fundamental difference, Bateman does share some qualities with Gatsby that should not be overlooked. Both model themselves slavishly on model images circulated by contemporary media. Nick Carraway, the narrator of Fitzgerald's novel, remarks that listening to Gatbsy is 'like skimming hastily through a dozen magazines' (Fitzgerald 1990: 54), while Daisy Buchanan tells Gatsby he resembles 'the advertisement of the man' (163). Similarly, in *American Psycho*, Bateman is referred to by his acquaintances as '*total GQ*' (Ellis 1997: 261). This label was embellished by Ellis in an interview when he described his protagonist as 'a mixture of *GQ* and *Stereo Review* and *Fangoria* [...] and *Vanity Fair*' (cited in Murphet 2002: 52). Bateman's ventriloquism is exhaustive. His voice resembles an echo chamber for consumer discourses: advertising jingles, fashion reportage, restaurant review, music journalism (during the chapter-long reviews of Genesis, Huey Lewis and Whitney Houston), technical reports on audiovisual equipment, talk show clichés, pornography and political sound bites: 'We have to end apartheid [...] And slow down the nuclear arms race, stop terrorism and world hunger' (41).

Before he begins to consume his victims, Bateman has himself already been consumed by the discourses of consumer capitalism. In a rare moment of insight into his own identity, Bateman recognizes that he does not have one: 'There is an idea of a Patrick Bateman;

some kind of abstraction. But there is no real me: only an entity, something illusory [...] I simply am not there' (362). There is no coherence or continuity to Bateman's frangible subjectivity since he merely reflects the images of others and then discards them like last season's fashion. Bateman masquerades as Donald Trump and magazine models from fashion shoots and as characters from various film genres. During sex with prostitutes he imagines himself as a porn star. In the chapter 'Chase, Manhattan', Bateman pictures himself as a criminal in an action film being pursued by the police while 'thinking there should be music' (336). Fleeing another crime scene, Bateman sees himself through the lens of a horror film camera: 'I'm running [...] screaming like a banshee, my coat open, flying out behind me like some kind of cape' (166). As a connoisseur of cult horror, Bateman is irked when a colleague mistakenly refers to the villain from *The Texas Chain Saw Massacre* (1974) as 'Feather head' rather than 'Leatherface'. He is also a devotee of historical serial killers: 'Bateman reads these biographies all the time: Ted Bundy and Son of Sam and *Fatal Vision* and Charlie Manson. All of them' (92). Bateman's lack of a distinctive identity extends beyond his wardrobe, home furnishings, musical tastes and political opinions to his serial killing. The violence in *American Psycho* represents a copycat homage to seminal horror icons: the sexual tortures of Ted Bundy, the Satanism of Son of Sam, the knife of Norman Bates (Bateman's near-namesake) from *Psycho* (1960), Jack Torrance's axe from *The Shining* (1980), Alex's power drill from *Body Double* and Leatherface's chainsaw. Numerous critics have rather casually proclaimed that Bateman is a serial killer, but *American Psycho* is carefully crafted to permit the possibility that all of the violence in fact belongs to Bateman's hyperactive fantasy life. The 'serial killer' could be another of the serial selves Bateman borrows from media culture to disguise the fact that he is 'simply not there'.

In *The Great Gatsby*, Nick Carraway speculates on the 'unreality of reality' and imagines that, for Gatsby, 'the rock of the world was founded securely on a fairy's wing' (Fitzgerald 1990: 112). *American Psycho* seems to share this sense that the material infrastructure of consumer society is based on images, dreams and fantasies. According to case studies, a hyperactive fantasy life is a key facet in the profile of the serial killer. It would be a mistake to dismiss these fantasies as merely the overture to violence; rather, the violence is a means of sustaining the fantasy. By the same token, the practice and pathology of serial consumerism is driven by fantasies from a collective phantasmagoria that cannot be finally fulfilled and so must be compulsively repeated. The hegemony of the visual in consumer culture is confirmed throughout *American Psycho*, both in the proliferation of images and visual technologies – network shows, movies, magazine and billboard ads, digital televisions, VCRs, cameras and camcorders – and in Bateman's concomitant tendency to see himself, others and the world through the camera's lens. The infamous images of violence in *American Psycho* might then need to be considered alongside the *violence of images* themselves. As Baudrillard suggests provocatively, 'the image [...] is violent because what happens there is the murder of the Real, the vanishing point of reality' (2003). In the world of 24/7 TV and cinema and videogames and advertising and computers and the internet, people become increasingly accustomed to consuming images of the world in place of the world itself. For Baudrillard these images initially frame and then replace reality with a vertiginous 'hyper-real' that refers only to itself. Although Baudrillard's speculations on the hegemony of the hyper-real have a seductive rhetorical force, we might need to pull back and consider that the dematerialization sketched in *American Psycho* is far from being a universal condition. The experience of consumer society as a realm in which commodities, places and subjects evaporate into signs, images and fantasies is in fact specific to particular classes and regions. This is the view, we might say, of Patrick Bateman and others who enjoy power and privilege in the postmodern playground. Those on the outside, both marginalized groups within the consumer society and the industrial proletariat manufacturing consumer goods in the developing world, remain urgently connected to material contingencies.

SHADOW BOXING IN *FIGHT CLUB*

Like Patrick Bateman, the narrator of *Fight Club* has a well-paid job, lives in a fashionable apartment and yet finds himself profoundly discontented, disconnected and hungry for violence. 'Joe's' job as a recall campaign coordinator for a car corporation requires travelling all over the country and yet his life seems essentially directionless. Suffering from insomnia he is prescribed an unusual course of treatment: 'My doctor said, if I wanted to see real pain, I should swing by First Eucharist on a

Tuesday night. See the brain parasites [...] See the cancer patients getting by' (Palahniuk 1999a: 19). 'Joe' feigns various illnesses to attend these support groups and this encounter with 'real pain' provides some relief. His recovery continues when he encounters a charismatic travelling soap salesman called Tyler Durden. After an explosion destroys the narrator's condominium, Tyler offers refuge in exchange for an unexpected request: 'I want you to hit me as hard as you can' (46). Following this inaugural act of violence more men get involved, the fighting goes underground – from parking lots to basements – clubs start to spring up across the country and branch out from bare-knuckle fighting to various pranks. Under Tyler's leadership, the club then develops into an increasingly militarized cult – 'Project Mayhem' – whose goal is nothing less than 'the complete and right-away destruction of civilization' (125). The narrator becomes anxious about the direction in which Tyler is leading his followers; however, at the point he decides to leave the club, 'Joe' makes the bizarre discovery that *he* is also Tyler. When 'Joe' realizes that 'Tyler Durden is [his] hallucination', the alter-ego mischievously retorts: 'Fuck that shit [...] Maybe you're *my* schizophrenic hallucination' (168). In *American Psycho*, Patrick Bateman (named after the schizophrenic Norman Bates from Hitchcock's *Psycho*) watches a special *Patty Winters Show* devoted to the subject of 'multiple personality vs. schizophrenia' (Ellis 1997: 286). Tantalizingly, Ellis leaves open the possibility that there might be *two* Patrick Batemans: the Wall Street financier and a fantasy self who dreams endlessly of violence. Ellis and Palahniuk dramatize split personality as a macabre Freudian cartoon and both connect their protagonist's 'psychogenic fugue[s]' and violence to consumerism (Palahniuk 1999a: 168). 'Joe's' doctor informs him that '[i]nsomnia is just the symptom of something larger. Find out what's actually wrong. Listen to your body' (19). By listening to his body, 'Joe' discovers that the 'something larger' causing his illness is consumer society itself.

Fight Club's unnamed narrator lives in an unnamed city which is saturated by the brand names of consumer capitalism:

The IBM Stellar Sphere.
The Philip Morris Galaxy.
Planet Denny's.

Every planet will take on the corporate identity of whoever rapes it first.
Budweiser World. (171)

After his apartment is destroyed, in a passage that rivals the brand bulimia of *American Psycho*, 'Joe' offers an inventory of his losses which is practically indistinguishable from an IKEA catalogue:

> my clever Njurunda coffee tables in the shape of a lime green yin and an orange yang that fit together to make a circle [...] My Haparanda sofa group with the orange slip covers, design by Erika Pekkari [...] the same Johanneshov armchair in the Strinne green stripe pattern. (43)

'Joe' fears that his desires are as manufactured and flimsy as flat-pack furniture. Despite the artful illusion of choice he has no real decision-making power: 'the Mommala quilt-cover set. Design by Tomas Harila and available in the following: Orchid. Fuchsia. Cobalt. Ebony. Jet. Eggshell or heather' (44). In the circumscribed spaces of consumerism, freedom might not mean much more than 'the freedom to choose between Brand X and Brand Y' (Lasch 1985: 38).

'Joe' realizes that his lack of real autonomy stems from a fundamental confusion between being and having. The attempt to perfect his home, car and wardrobe has become the core of his identity: 'That was my whole life. Everything, the lamps, the chairs, the rugs were me. The dishes in the cabinets were me. The plants were me. The television was me' (Palahniuk 1999a: 111). 'Joe' feels increasingly indistinguishable from and imprisoned by his possessions:

> It took my whole life to buy this stuff [...] Buy the sofa [...] Then the right set of dishes. Then the perfect bed. The drapes. The rug. Then you're trapped in your lovely nest, and the things you used to own, now they own you. (44)

The sense of incarceration is augmented by accompanying descriptions of 'Joe's' luxury condo as 'a sort of filing cabinet for widows and young professionals [...] a foot of concrete, ceiling and wall [...] you couldn't open the windows' (41). 'Joe' feels constricted and compartmentalized both at home and in his working life. His job as a 'young professional' involves continuous business travel: 'You wake up at O'Hare. You wake up at LaGuardia. You wake up at Logan' (25). The people 'Joe' meets appear to be mere adjuncts to the commodity world: 'single-serving friends' (21) to complement the 'tiny soaps, tiny shampoos, single-serving butter, tiny mouthwash' he receives on flights and in hotels (31). 'Joe's' relationship with commodities threatens to replace his relationship with other people and he begins to suspect that consumerism has even become a substitute for sex: 'The people I know who used to sit in the bathroom with pornography, now they sit in the bathroom with their IKEA furniture catalogue' (43). This remark resonates with Norman Mailer's claim that sex and consumerism have coalesced:

> Talk of pornography ought to begin at the modern root: *advertising*. Ten years ago the advertisements sold the girl with the car – the not altogether unfair connection of the unconscious mind was that the owner of a new convertible was on the way to getting a new girl. Today the girl means less than the machine. A car is sold not because it will help one to get a girl, but because it already is a girl. (1992b: 431)

'Joe's' alienation from himself and other people is interlaced with his fetishistic dependency on a system of consumer objects which, as in *American Psycho*, is itself being consumed by images. As is evident in the conversion of his apartment into a simulacral shrine to Swedish home furnishing, 'Joe' invests less in material objects than in the image of things. Like Patrick Bateman, the narrator at the outset of *Fight Club* models his life, his clothing and interior design on images from television and film, magazines and catalogues. In this context, Stuart Ewen has written about the 'extreme alienation' that results when:

> frozen images – in ads or style magazines – become the models from which people design their living spaces or themselves [...] The extent to which objects seem so promising may be an index of the extent to which the human subject is in jeopardy; destined only to be a consumer. (1990: 91)

'Joe' is trapped inside the gilded cage of a hyper-reality in which '[e]verything is so far away, a copy of a copy of a copy' (Palahniuk 1999a: 21). The Tyler Durden part of 'Joe's' personality links this alienation to advertising which 'has these people chasing cars and clothes they don't need' (149). Advertising produces hyper-real simulations and generates artificial desires, but Tyler promises to 'deliver [us] from Swedish furniture' (46). Against the common-sense assumption that commodities are produced because consumers need them, *Fight Club* counters with the assertion that a certain type of consumer subjectivity is produced because it is needed by the commodity system. Palahniuk asks us to consider the possibility that the most important product in the consumer society is *the consumer*.

'Joe' goes through several stages in his attempt to break free from this scripted subjectivity and a life that feels somnabulatory and synthetic. His initial response involves leaving behind the 'lovely nest' for the support groups at First Eucharist. Facing the reality of illness and death allows 'Joe' an intimacy and intensity of experience which is painfully absent from his everyday life: 'Walking home after the support group, I felt more alive than I'd ever felt' (22). While everything else around him feels counterfeit – 'a copy of a copy of a copy' (21) – Chloe, a woman he meets who has terminal cancer, is 'the genuine article' (36). This newfound sense of authenticity is jeopardized, however, when another imposter, Marla, arrives and holds up a mirror to 'Joe's' own fakery: 'all of a sudden even death and dying rank right down there with plastic flowers on video as a non-event' (23). 'Joe's' first 'meeting' with Tyler comes soon after Marla's disruptive intrusion. Having lost the refuge of the support groups, Tyler offers 'Joe' an alternative and more confrontational means of escaping consumer society. Tyler's tactics involve an eclectic blend of adolescent pranks, culture-jamming as practised by anti-consumerist groups and carnivalesque subversion. In place of the slick and sanitized mannequin model, Tyler offers to return the body to a messy materialism: he mixes bodily fluids into food in exclusive restaurants; as a cinema projectionist he inserts subliminal images of genitalia from porn into family films; and he recycles human fat to sell it back as designer soap to the same women who have liposuction treatments. While advertising idealizes the consumer as a 'beautiful and unique snowflake', Tyler offers a dissenting vision of the body as 'decaying organic matter [...] we are all part of the same compost pile' (126).

The main tactic Tyler uses to return the numbed consumer body to its abject origins is violence. The fight club encourages its participants to abandon the ephemeral pleasures of consumption for the concrete reality of physical pain: '"Come back to the pain", Tyler says' (67). While consumer culture revolves around a virtualized visuality, the fight club privileges the tactile sense by seeking to reconnect the combatants with their own and other bodies. In the hyper-mediated phantasmagoria of consumerism 'you can't touch anything and nothing can touch you', but Tyler initiates the fight club by asking the narrator to 'hit me as hard as you can' (46). Tyler valorizes the physical intimacy of violent contact and the marks which it leaves on the body – the cuts, bruises and scars. 'Joe's' hand is disfigured by lye in the shape of Tyler's kiss and the 'Space Monkeys' use the same solution to burn off their fingerprints. *Fight Club* thus stages a combative confrontation between, in one corner, a subversive self (a '[p]ost consumer human butt wipe' (109) that is primarily tactile, scarred and anonymous (missing fingerprints)) and in the other the consumer subject (with his flawless, soap-scrubbed skin and the illusory aura of a 'sacred, unique snowflake of special unique specialness' (199)). Tyler's proposition that '[m]aybe self-improvement isn't the answer [...] Maybe self-destruction is the answer' (49), is aimed less at literal suicide than the elimination of all traces of the consumer self. His radical solution to the problem of overpowering consumerism is to destroy the system as it is embodied in you.

In part, Tyler's recourse to violence is a mimetic response to the structural violence of the system he aims to overthrow. *Fight Club* itself aims to incite critical consideration of *where* commodities come from, *what* they are made from and *how* they are made: to smell glamorous perfumes and think about 'dead whales' (84); to see 'tanning spray' and think about cutting the eyelids off animals in toxicity tests (86). 'Joe' suggests at one point that '[i]f you know where to look, there are bodies buried everywhere' (126). The soap manufactured by the Paper Street Company symbolizes the dirty secrets and hidden histories that can lie beneath the surface of commodities – Tyler's prestige beauty product is made out of fat sucked from 'the fattest, wealthiest thighs in America' and then mixed with herbs grown in a garden of 'dirt and hair and shit and bone and blood' (136). At times, however, Tyler's ripostes seem motivated less by a determination to eliminate the structural violence of consumerism than a desire to exceed it: '[b]urn the Amazon rain forests. Pump chlorofluorocarbons straight up to gobble the ozone.

Open the dump valves on supertankers and uncap offshore oil wells' (123).

Alongside some carefully picked punches against consumerism, Tyler engages in wild flailing against all of western civilization. As well as planning to bring the world's tallest skyscraper down on top of the National Museum, Tyler wants 'to burn the Louvre. [To] do the Elgin marbles with a sledgehammer and wipe my ass with the Mona Lisa' (124). While these aspirations might be redeemed as an assault on the commercialism of the culture and heritage industries, we should note that Tyler's rhetorical assault on mother nature and the Mona Lisa is part of a wider onslaught against the feminine. At times in *Fight Club* it appears as though consumerism and civilization are merely the agents that deliver the virus of femininity. Tyler rails against matriarchal domination and subsequent emasculation of 'a generation of men raised by women' (50). 'Big Bob', a gym owner who develops 'bitch tits' after the removal of his testicles, represents a literal symbol of this figurative castration (9). Tyler offers to take the soft and blubbery American male and make him hard again: men hugging and crying in support groups will be replaced by men hitting each other in a fight club. At First Eucharist, the narrator leaves the imprint of his face in tears on Bob's T-shirt while at the fight club there is 'a print of half ['Joe's'] face in blood on the floor' (51). While the support group is all about talking through your problems, the fight club restores traditional masculine reticence. The first and the second rules are 'you don't talk about fight club': 'Fight Club isn't about words [...] there's grunting and noise [...] there's hysterical shouting in tongues like at church' (51). 'Joe's' experiences at fight club go beyond athletic confrontation into the apparently mystical realm of ancient patriarchal rituals in which blood must be spilt.

According to Tyler, men are genetically-programmed hunters who have been ensnared and neutered by a feminizing consumer culture. Traditionally, within the sexual division of labour under capitalism, men have dominated production and work while women have been assigned to consumption and the domestic sphere. Contemporary consumer society has seen a withering of long-established gender polarities. Most women now work outside the home and increasing numbers of men participate in consumer practices while losing touch with the world of production and physical labour which undergirded traditional definitions of muscular masculinity. This is the predicament in which the narrator of *Fight Club* finds himself. 'Joe' is a pampered consumer obsessed with feathering his 'lovely nest' (36). Tyler, however, destroys 'Joe's' apartment and aims to replace the 'nesting instinct' with old-fashioned patriarchal pursuits. The wit, energy and charisma of 'Joe's' alter-ego should not, however, blind us to the fact that Tyler's version of 'old-fashioned' is practically prehistoric. Project Mayhem aims to turn the clocks back not merely to the days before consumer culture and feminism, but to the days before there were clocks. Tyler promises his disciples that they will:

> hunt elk through the damp canyon forests around the ruins of the Rockefeller Centre, and dig clams next to the skeleton of the Space Needle [...] stalking elk past department store windows and stinking racks of beautiful rotting dresses and tuxedos on hangers; you'll wear leather clothes that will last you the rest of your life, and you'll climb the wrist-thick kudzu vines that wrap the Sears Tower. (116)

Amidst the ruins of the phallic towers of commerce (Rockefeller Centre), technology (the Space Needle) and consumerism (the Sears Tower), American men will rebuild an archaic masculinity. The reborn US male will leave behind the gilded cage of emasculating consumerism (the 'department store [with its] stinking racks of beautiful rotting dresses') and ornamental masculinity ('tuxedos on hangers') to don leather clothing in the great outdoors (which echoes Leatherstocking, James Fenimore Cooper's mythic archetype of American masculinity).

'THIS IS NOT AN EXIT'?

Tyler offers to lead disenchanted American men from the matriarchal malls of consumer society back into the great outdoors where they can recover a mythic masculinity. Crucially, however, the authority of Tyler's vision diminishes as the ranks of Project Mayhem swell. 'Joe' begins to distance himself from the Project as it builds into a paramilitary cadre that replicates the lack of autonomy and individuality previously associated with corporate and consumer drones. But why does the anti-consumerist politics in *Fight Club* snowball into black-shirted and boot-clicking fascism? We might find a clue in an interview Palahniuk gave in 1999 when he was asked directly if 'consumerism is bad [...] what is good?' The author dodged this question with evasive irony: 'I want to sidestep that one. Seriously, buy my book. Or better yet, send me gobs of money. Please don't make me wrestle that intellectual greased pig anymore' (Palahniuk 1999b). Palahniuk's sense that the critique of consumerism is vexed and slippery was undoubtedly reinforced by the 'gobs of money' he made from worldwide sales of his anti-consumerist novel. In fact, the interview in which he was confronted with this question was part of a promotional campaign which coincided with the release of a blockbuster Hollywood adaptation of his cult book.

The consumption of literature is a global multi-million dollar industry that itself provides a crucial context for any consideration of the literary critique of consumerism. This context extends into a variety of commercial spin-offs: sales of Palahniuk's novel since 1999 – significantly re-titled *Fight Club: A Novel* in some editions – were significantly boosted by David Fincher's 1999 film adaptation (to which we will return in Chapter 7), which in turn spawned a soundtrack CD, posters, T-shirts and a videogame. When Ellis's *American Psycho* was adapted as a film by Mary Harron in 2000 the spin-offs included an action figure dressed in a fake mini-Armani suit and armed with a carving knife. US popular culture since the early 90s has witnessed an increasing fascination with violent crime in general and serial killing in particular. The transformation of murder and grisly torture into a spectacle for visual consumption testifies to the phenomenal capacity of capitalism to convert almost any subject or object into a commodity. The incorporative power of consumer capitalism can even extend to anti-consumerist politics as dissent is appropriated, repackaged and sold back to society as fashionable subcultural dissidence. In his influential analysis of postmodernism, the American Marxist critic Fredric Jameson bemoans the 'abolition of critical distance': any artist or critic who opposes consumer capitalism is at risk of being 'somehow secretly disarmed and reabsorbed by a system of which they themselves might well be considered a part since they can achieve no distance from it' (1991: 57). Jameson's assertion that there might no longer be a viable 'outside' to the system resonates with the final sentence in *American Psycho* which has Patrick Bateman transfixed by a sign that says 'THIS IS NOT AN EXIT' (384). The commercial success of Ellis and Palahniuk's fiction also appears to reinforce Jameson's dire warning about the commodification of critique. Are novelists, then, capable of no more than merely scratching (profitably) at the shiny and impervious surfaces of consumer culture? We would like to conclude by suggesting that the prognosis might not be quite as dismal as Jameson's pronouncement suggests.

To begin with, we might challenge the stark antithesis of 'critique' and 'commodification'. This opposition is reductive since it erases significant degrees of complicity and resistance. No opponent of consumerism would dare to imagine that a critical commentary on IKEA furniture in a contemporary novel would lead instantly to the collapse of a multinational corporation. By the same token, one should not leap to the conclusion that the slightest hint of commercialism automatically eradicates the oppositional potential of any critique. While *Fight Club* may be guilty of a rather polished packaging of oppositional politics, its commercial success does not provide a wholesale invalidation of the diverse forms of radical anti-consumerism currently being practised around the world by workers' movements and environmentalists, anti-globalization groups and anarchist organizations – even those, such as CrimethInc. or the anarcho-primitivists, whose political vision is echoed in the rhetoric of Tyler Durden. Rather than assuming that commodification in one area of society inevitably abrogates critique *per se*, we might consider the possibility that the incursions of commodification make critique even more urgently essential.

In *Empire* (2001), their seminal study of the globalization of capital, Hardt and Negri propose that if 'there is no longer a place that can be recognized as outside, we must be against in every place' (2001: 210). The 'will to be against' is evident throughout *American Psycho* and *Fight Club*. This oppositional imperative is manifest not only in the multiple transgressions of their protagonists, but in the very form of the novels themselves. As part of their effort to be 'against' consumerism both novels are also 'against' themselves as part of the system they would oppose. Palahniuk's novel is doubly conflicted since it is focalized through a split personality – a character who is literally against himself and whose opposition to consumerism echoes the enervating language of sound bites, spectacles and products. Ellis's novel offers an even more resound-ingly hollow mimicry of the discourses of consumerism. *American Psycho* is a wilfully numbing anti-novel which attempts to short-circuit the commodification of critique by deliriously performing its own commodification. Somewhat perversely, perhaps, we might say that critique appears here as its own gravitational absence – a black hole that implodes towards an end that is 'NOT AN EXIT'.

CHAPTER FOUR

BETWEEN BLACK AND WHITE

BELOVED (1987) AND *THE HUMAN STAIN* (2000)

Fictions of race

As Toni Morrison notes in *Playing in the Dark*, the United States is 'a highly and historically racialized society' (1993: 4). Race, therefore, is not simply one topic among others in US fiction but a subject that is inescapably present. Recent scholarly work on race has been concerned to 'denaturalize' racial categories: underlining the extent to which 'race' is a regulatory fiction that we bring to the world rather than something that we find in it. Far from a transparent and timeless category denoting a fixed and unchanging biological or cultural essence, race is a contingent and historical classificatory framework that has functioned primarily to perform the ideological operation of separating 'insider' from 'outsider', 'us' from 'them.' Racial thinking, on this argument, *produces* rather than describes group differences. This critique of 'essentialist' notions of race, emphasizing its status as a 'social construction', offers opportunities and risks. Morrison has expressed a note of scepticism in her seminal essay, 'Unspeakable Things Unspoken':

> For three hundred years black Americans insisted that 'race' was no usefully distinguishing factor in human relationships. During those same three centuries every academic discipline, including theology, history, and natural science, insisted 'race' was *the* determining factor in human development. When blacks discovered they had shaped or become a culturally formed race, and that it had specific and revered difference, suddenly they were told there is no such thing as 'race,' biological or cultural,

that matters and that genuinely intellectual exchange cannot accommodate it. [...] It always seemed to me that the people who invented the hierarchy of 'race' when it was convenient for them ought not to be the ones to explain it away, now that it does not suit their purposes for it to exist. (1989: 3)

If denaturalizing race threatens to complicate (and entails a re-description of) projects of racial pride, it also promises, not to 'explain away' racial hierarchies, but to illuminate and unpick those ideological operations that have enabled their construction and repetition. It should be stressed that scholarly emphasis on the social construction of race in no way implies that race somehow vanishes. Race, as Dominick LaCapra has put it, is 'a feeble mystification with formidable effects' (1991: 1).

Morrison's *Beloved* (1987) and Philip Roth's *The Human Stain* (2000) are two very different recent novelistic explorations of the mystifications and effects of race. In different ways, both novels confirm Morrison's insight that 'in spite of its implicit or explicit acknowledgement, "race" is still a virtually unspeakable thing' (1989: 3). Along with gender and class, race was mobilized as a central category in the culture wars of the 1980s and 1990s, and both novels explore race, and the relationship between race and national identity, in ways that are influenced by and join debates over multiculturalism and identity politics. Together, *Beloved* and *The Human Stain* indicate that, far from resembling a 'post-racial' society, the US remains haunted by race.

Morrison's status in contemporary American culture is encouragingly multiple and ambiguous – at once Nobel laureate and frequent sitter on Oprah's sofa, cloistered academic and impassioned public commentator on such matters as the O. J. Simpson trial in 1995. This determined public participation refuses to indulge notions of the novelist as reclusive, alienated outsider whose nuanced insights are fated to go unheard in a kinetic and commodified public sphere. In *The Human Stain*, by contrast, Roth invokes such clichés in a way that at once critiques and retains them. Nathan Zuckerman, Roth's longstanding writer narrator, isolates himself from his peers in order to focus entirely on writing. In fact, his discovery that 'the trick to living alone [...] away from all agitating entanglements' is 'to organize the silence, to think of its mountaintop plenitude as capital' (Roth 2001: 44) already complicates notions of writerly solitude by aligning Zuckerman's creativity with the economic growth of the Clinton years. Eventually, however, Zuckerman renounces such solitude; the production of his novel – also called *The Human Stain* – enacts a return to 'the jumble, the mayhem, the mess' of the social, albeit with the implied hope of producing a 'disturbance' in its consciousness (3).

Beloved also seeks to disturb. In part, Morrison's public engagement draws upon and extends the theory and practice of the Black Arts Movement of the 1960s, with its urgent emphasis upon art as a resolutely political act. For the artists and writers forging and recovering a 'black aesthetic', the misguided separation of art and politics – 'art for art's sake' – belonged to a hegemonic and harmful white European aesthetic. In 'Black Cultural Nationalism', for example, Ron Karenga argued that African American cultural production 'must have three basic characteristics which make it revolutionary. In brief, it must be functional, collective and committing' (1968: 6). To be functional, or 'useful', such art 'must expose the enemy, praise the people and support the revolution' (6); to be collective, 'it must be from the people and returned to the people in a form more colourful and beautiful than everyday life' (7); to be committing, it 'must commit us to revolution and change. It must commit us to a future that is ours' (9).

As Karenga's rhetoric of 'revolution' reminds us, the cultural work of the Black Arts Movement ran parallel to the Black Power Movement of the 1960s. Inevitably, then, there are both continuities and discontinuities between Morrison's novelistic practice and Karenga's aesthetic strategies for cultural nationalism. Morrison's continuity with the black aesthetic is suggested by the conviction that her work is 'demonstrably inseparable from a cultural specificity that is Afro-American' (Morrison 1989: 19). Since Morrison's work also underscores the hybridity of US culture as a whole – the fact that it is inseparably marked by several cultural specificities and must work conspicuously hard to suggest otherwise – this need not be taken to imply a narrowly nationalist agenda.

Although Morrison's public celebrity may seem to soften generalized doubts about the continued relevance of the novel in a culture readily identified as post-novelistic, it should be noted that the efficacy of the novel as a mode of cultural production is nevertheless at issue for her. Paul Gilroy has described the formal distinctiveness of *Beloved* as reflecting 'discomfort' with the novel as a form, stemming from 'anxiety about its utility as a resource in the social processes that govern the remaking and conservation of historical memory' (1993: 218–19). In conversation with Gilroy, Morrison contends that the novel form 'is needed [...] now in a way that it was not needed before', in that it offers a useful, relatively autonomous discursive space for African American artists by comparison with traditional musical forms of black cultural production that have been thoroughly appropriated:

> For a long time, the art form that was healing for black people was music. That music is no longer exclusively ours; we don't have exclusive rights to it. Other people sing and play it, it is the mode of contemporary music everywhere. So another form has to take its place, and it seems to me that the novel is needed [...] now in a way that it was not needed before. (Gilroy 1993: 219)

The novel remains a useful resource for Morrison just because its ideological and formal content is still an open question, allowing for both experimentation and intervention.

With Karenga's aesthetic template in mind, we might say that 'the enemy' *Beloved* seeks to expose is the national amnesia surrounding the history and legacy of African and African American slavery. Morrison has described that determined and contradictory forgetfulness in compelling terms:

> We live in a land where the past is always erased and America is the innocent future in which immigrants can come and start over, where the slate is clean. The past is absent or it's romanticized. This culture doesn't encourage dwelling on, let alone coming to terms with, the truth about the past. (Gilroy 1993: 222)

The Human Stain's main protagonist exploits just this amnesiac mythology in order to obscure his African American origins and 'start over' by claiming to be a second-generation immigrant whose Russian Jewish ancestry has conveniently faded. In doing so, he jettisons an extensive family genealogy that is already richly American. The revealing contradiction here is that an African American character invokes the myths of emigration in order to sidestep racial inequality and 'join' the society of which he is already a fundamental part.

Beloved confronts amnesiac notions of America as *tabula rasa* and undertakes a coming to terms with the national past, beginning with its dedication to the 'Sixty Million and More' victims of the Middle Passage and US slavery. The narrative centres on a resistant ('rough') assertion of agency and humanity based on historical records of Margaret Garner. In 1856, after escaping slavery in Kentucky by crossing the frozen Ohio River, Garner cut the throat of one of her daughters when confronted by slave catchers, rather than have her captured and returned to slavery. Garner's case was taken up by the anti-slavery abolitionist movement – its suggestion that death would be preferable to slavery provided luminous proof of the absolute inhumanity of slavery as an institution. Proponents of slavery, meanwhile, recruited Garner's action as further justification of slavery – as *Beloved* renders their paternalistic arguments, 'testimony to the results of a little so-called freedom imposed on people who needed every care and guidance in the world to keep them from the cannibal life they preferred' (Morrison 1987: 177). Morrison's novel was inspired in part by a contemporary account of the Garner incident from the *American Baptist* included in *The Black Book*, a companion to African American history that Morrison edited when working for the publishers Random House. The author of the account, P. S. Bassett, describes a visit to Garner in prison:

> She said that when the officers and slave-hunters came to the house in which they were concealed, she caught a shovel and struck two of her children on the head, and then took a knife and cut the throat of the third, and tried to kill the other, – that if they had given her time, she would have killed them all – that with regard to herself, she cared but little; but she was unwilling to have her children suffer as she had done. (Harris 1974: 10)

The 'officers and slave-hunters' were acting legally within the framework of the Fugitive Slave Act of 1850, which mandated the return of runaway slaves to their masters as so much missing property.

Beloved stages a fictional, narrative refashioning of Garner's action, returning the reader to the brutal history of US slavery in a way that draws on the perspectives and issues enabled and identified by contemporary black feminism. Stuart Hall's essay 'Cultural

Identity and Cinematic Representation' provides some useful terms with which to describe this aspect of Morrison's novel. *Beloved* works to provide a '*re-telling* of the past' that simultaneously involves the rediscovery and the production of identity, a claiming of absences (Hall 1996: 212). Morrison's text imagines a voice for Garner and for the black bodies lost in the Middle Passage in a fictional retrieval and act of willed remembering that is inherently political, establishing urgent connections between the past and the present. After Sethe tells Paul D of how she 'put my babies where they'd be safe', he reflects:

> This here Sethe was new. [...] This here Sethe talked about love like any other woman; talked about baby clothes like any other woman, but what she meant could cleave the bone. This here Sethe talked about safety with a handsaw. This here new Sethe didn't know where the world stopped and she began. Suddenly he saw what Stamp Paid wanted him to see: more important than what Sethe had done was what she claimed. It scared him. (Morrison 1987: 193)

Paul D's sense of Sethe's newness records his troubled realization of her strength and independence, but that newness is also a function of *Beloved*'s retrieval of Garner's story through contemporary feminist paradigms. And these paradigms, in turn, extend to the mid-nineteenth-century feminist movement in the US, as represented for example by the Declaration of Sentiments issuing from the Seneca Falls Convention in 1848. Quite aside from its psychoanalytical associations, Sethe's not knowing where the world stops and she begins signifies Morrison's textual arrogation for Sethe of agency and subjectivity. This proves an anxious claim for Paul D, given his recurrent doubts over his masculine autonomy, and resists those narrative perspectives imposed on Sethe by both Schoolteacher and Paul D that question her humanity ('"You got two feet, Sethe, not four"' (1987: 194)).

In undertaking a 'critical engagement with history' (Perez-Torres 1999: 183), *Beloved* runs against the grain of early and influential theorizations of literary postmodernism, in which novels – along with cultural forms in general – were seen to evince an absence of historical consciousness matching the amnesia of late twentieth-century consumer society. *Beloved*'s historical focus, however, complicates straightforwardly referential notions of historical representation by addressing 'things ... halfway told' (Morrison 1987: 45), not just the gaps and absences in the historical record but the experiential and historical trauma of slavery. Roger Luckhurst persuasively identifies *Beloved* as a 'paradigmatic' trauma fiction (2008: 91). Slavery is represented in *Beloved* as an experience or condition that not only overwhelms and fractures subjectivity but also 'disarticulates linear narrative' representation (Luckhurst 2008: 91). As such, Morrison's novel necessarily deploys a series of complex formal strategies in order to realize its premise of slave subjectivity and agency. *Beloved* often employs metonymic part–whole relationships, for example, because the whole is unapproachable. If *Beloved* is informed by identity politics, then, the difficulty of the text is that the identities in question are severely traumatized or wounded – it takes almost the entire novel, for example, for Sethe to arrive at the possibility of a self-assertion that is more than 'the potent pride of the mistreated' (Morrison 1997: 112), and even then such assertion takes the form of a question: '"Me? Me?"' (322).

In terms of narrative form, a principal way in which *Beloved* figures the traumatized subjectivities of its several protagonists is through the frequent deployment of flashback. The narrative present of *Beloved* is set in Cincinnati, Ohio between 1873 and 1874, after the Civil War, therefore, and eighteen years after Sethe's 'rough choice' in 1855, the taking of her baby daughter's life that ends her twenty-eight days of 'having women friends, a mother-in-law, and all her children together; of being part of a neighborhood' (205). *Beloved* begins with Sethe suspended in the narrative present between an overwhelming and repressed past and a future that is therefore foreclosed. Engaged daily in the 'serious work of beating back the past' (86), Sethe is haunted by the return of the repressed, with memories interrupting her consciousness and the linearity of Morrison's narrative. Sethe is only able to reclaim the present and future by confronting or working through her memories, not individually but collectively through and with the community. If we see Sethe's task as one of fashioning a narrative that allows her, as Mae G. Henderson puts it, 'to demonstrate her possession *of* rather than *by* the past' (1999: 99), then the analogy with Morrison's own task in *Beloved* becomes clear: to confront the present with the history of slavery that has been repressed or 'disremembered'. This cannot, of course, consist in an imaginative reunification but rather in an open-ended call for the reader to take up the text's difficult work of memory.

If the temporal shifts attaching to characters' recollections produce one kind of disruption for the reader, another sort can be found on the novel's opening page. Morrison has written of how, by placing readers *in media res* with the first sentence of *Beloved*, she intended their epistemological situation – their lack of orientation within the fictional world of the text – to somewhat parallel the disorientation of the slave experience:

> The reader is snatched, yanked, thrown into an environment completely foreign, and I want it as the first stroke of the shared experience that might be possible between the reader and the novel's population. Snatched just as the slaves were from one place to another, without preparation and without defense. (1989: 32)

In his influential study of *The Black Atlantic*, Paul Gilroy argues that the signature aesthetic and social experiences associated with early twentieth-century European modernity and modernism – the fragmentation of subjectivity, narrative and history – were experienced by blacks at least a century earlier by virtue of their subjection to the racial terror of slavery. It is black slavery and diaspora, Gilroy argues, that mark the historical beginnings of modernity:

> the concentrated intensity of the slave experience is something that marked out blacks as the first truly modern people, handling in the nineteenth century dilemmas and difficulties which would only become the substance of everyday life in Europe a century later. (1993: 221)

The disorienting formal devices of literary modernism – its experiments with perspective and temporality – get deployed in *Beloved* in a paradoxically realist or mimetic spirit as a means of indicating the terror of slavery.

In addition to reactivating literary modernism, *Beloved* also employs a central motif from white-authored American Gothic literature of the nineteenth century: the haunted house. This is something other than a simple appropriation since, as Morrison has argued elsewhere, canonical American writers such as Edgar

Allan Poe were always already negotiating issues of race and slavery in their work. 124 Bluestone Road is haunted by the ghost of Sethe's murdered daughter, Beloved, as Paul D discovers when he encounters 'a pool of red undulating light' on entering the house (1987: 10). Baby Suggs's response to Sethe's suggestion that they leave the house to escape the ghost is instructive: ' "What'd be the point? [...] Not a house in the country ain't packed to its rafters with some dead Negro's grief" ' (6). With this response, *Beloved* early on establishes the ghostly as a way of figuring the national haunting of slavery.

The superficially disturbing novelties of the ghostly invoke, but also give way to, the far more disturbing psychological and corporeal *realities* of slavery. As Morrison notes:

> The fully realized presence of the haunting is both a major incumbent of the narrative and sleight of hand. One of its purposes is to keep the reader preoccupied with the nature of the incredible spirit world while being supplied a controlled diet of the incredible political world. (1989: 32)

After Paul D forces the ghost out of 124, it reappears in the form of a young woman, Beloved. The hermeneutic status of Beloved is irrevocably multiple, and must be understood in both/and rather than either/or terms. As 'the girl who waited to be loved and cry shame' (1987: 323), Beloved is Sethe's daughter come back to life, although, as Denver puts it after Beloved's departure, 'At times I think she was – more' (314). Beloved is also the girl Stamp Paid describes who had been 'locked up in the house with a whiteman over by Deer Creek' (277). And as becomes evident in the sections of the text focalized from 'her' narrative perspective, Beloved also represents the collective voice of those subjected to the Middle Passage, 'crouching and watching others who are crouching too' in a slave ship (248).

Beloved insists throughout on the 'incredible' character of the political world by following the example of Sethe's 'rough response to the Fugitive Bill' (201) and depicting characters refusing to normalize and thereby legitimize the world they inhabit. Central to *Beloved* is its depiction of the violence done to kinship structures by slavery:

> all of Baby's life, as well as Sethe's own, men and women were moved around like checkers. Anybody Baby Suggs knew, let

alone loved, who hadn't run off or been hanged, got rented out, loaned out, bought up, brought back, stored up, mortgaged, won, stolen or seized. So Baby's eight children had six fathers. What she called the nastiness of life was the shock she received upon learning that nobody stopped playing checkers just because the pieces included her children. (27–8)

The struggle to maintain and recover such relationships is seen in the novel to run up against severe and systematic violence, both literal and ideological – from the way that slavery undoes mother–child relations by treating the children of slaves as commodities to the refusal of slaveholders to conceive of relationships between slaves in terms of family structures. *Beloved* condenses such violence with its account of Schoolteacher's two nephews holding Sethe down at Sweet Home and stealing the milk from her breasts, frustrating her anxious desire to get her milk to her 'crawling-already' baby at 124. The scars on Sethe's back, described by Amy as forming 'a choke-cherry tree' (93), are inflicted when the nephews learn that Sethe has told Mrs. Garner of their action. Family relationships between slaves are also subject to linguistic violence, with the imposition of slave names further obscuring family connections and thereby enabling the treatment of slaves as objects rather than subjects.

By tarrying over the logic of Sethe's infanticide, *Beloved* refuses to naturalize the 'incredible political world' of nineteenth-century slavery; in the dehumanizing context of institutional slavery – 'the world done up the way whitefolks loved it' (222) – Sethe's apparently inhumane action can be understood as an act of humanity. Denver's interior monologue tells us that, although 'there sure is something in her that makes it all right to kill her own', she also understands that 'the thing that made it all right for my mother to kill my sister [...] comes from outside this house, outside the yard' (242). Denver's reflections here speak of the problematic narrowing of her world to 124, but they also refuse to pathologize Sethe's action by correctly locating its genesis as an external imposition. We find the same refusal in the text's gradual suggestion that the community of her peers has shunned Sethe not out of disgust over her action – which is all too understandable – but through intolerance of her prideful attempt to manage alone. The assistance that Amy offers to Sethe is also key here, in that the cooperation of these 'two throw-away people' is figured as both the projection and the resumption of an undistorted unity, in which class and gender alliances transcend racial divides: 'There was nothing to disturb them at their work. So they did it appropriately and well' (100). A marked and resistant lack of false consciousness is evident in the text's African American characters, from Stamp Paid's self-naming to Baby Suggs's private rejection of Garner's suggestion that his allowing Halle to buy out his mother's service (and thereby free her) mitigates the character of slavery: 'But you got my boy and I'm all broke down. You be renting him out to pay for me long after I'm gone to Glory' (174).

Emancipation is depicted in *Beloved* as thoroughly ambivalent and equivocal in character: 'The War had been over four or five years then, but nobody white or black seemed to know it' (63). More hopefully, Denver's 'step off the edge of the world' of 124 (286), her eventual re-entry into the community to ask for help, suggests a positive future: 'She was shocked to see how small the big things were: the boulder by the edge of the road she once couldn't see over was a sitting-on rock. Paths leading to houses weren't miles long' (289). Such new perspectives are complicated by the money holder Denver notices in the Bodwins' house, a grotesque caricature of an African American atop a pedestal reading 'At Yo Service' (300). Its presence confirms Sethe's sense that slavery, although ended, remains a threat for Denver, and suggests both an uncertain economic future and the critical, cultural task ahead of refusing damaging stereotypes, a task embraced in the 1920s, for example, by the African American modernism of the Harlem Renaissance.

Beloved reminds us of something that Coleman Silk discovers in *The Human Stain*: that 'definitions belong to the definers – not the defined' (Morrison 1987: 222). Slaves and slave owners are both depicted in the novel as questioning one another's humanity, with the slaveholders justifying their ownership and treatment of slaves by regarding their property as less than human. Absolutely central to the practice of slavery is the ideological assumption on the part of the slaveholder that the slave is without history, without culture, and without humanity. For the former slaves, meanwhile, the barbarity of the heterogeneous practices of slavery cast severe doubt on the humanity of the slaveholders – making it a doubtful assumption at best. As Stamp Paid asks, after finding 'a red ribbon knotted around a curl of wet woolly hair, clinging to its bit of scalp' floating in the river, '"What *are* these people? You tell me, Jesus. What *are* they' (213); or, as Baby Suggs advises her granddaughter, 'even when they [whites] thought they were being human, it was a far cry from what real humans did' (287).

With *Beloved*, Morrison seeks to memorialize black genocide in the United States. As such, the novel inevitably involves a less than comforting address to the white reader in its excavation of what Morrison refers to as the 'predatory western phenomena' of slavery, a phenomenon involving the degradation of whites no less than blacks. Writing in his *Notes on the State of Virginia* (1785), future US President Thomas Jefferson was acutely aware that the slave owner's personality 'cannot but be stamped by it [slavery] with odious peculiarities' (1977: 214). As Morrison argues:

> You can call it an ideology and an economy, what it is is a pathology. Slavery broke the world in half, it broke it in every way. It broke Europe. It made them into something else, it made them slave masters, it made them crazy. You can't do that for hundreds of years and it not take a toll. They had to dehumanize, not just the slaves but themselves. They have had to reconstruct everything in order to make that system appear true. It made everything in world war two possible. It made world war one necessary. Racism is the word that we use to encompass all this. (Gilroy 1993: 221)

Familiar and clichéd journalistic formulations of modernism as responding to an absurd world without meaning take on an unexpected sense here, giving way to a world turned upside down in order to habituate and make normal the selling and ownership of black bodies. It is the fundamental perversity of slavery that informs and accounts for such paradoxical formulations in *Beloved* as Sethe's reflection that 'if I hadn't killed her she would have died and that is something I could not bear to happen to her' (Morrison 1997: 236). Morrison's comments also offer a fruitful perspective on Stanley Crouch's notorious claim, in his dismissive review, that *Beloved* 'is a blackface holocaust novel. It seems to have been written in order to enter American slavery into the big-time martyr ratings contest, a contest usually won by references to, and remarks about, the experience of the Jews at the hands of Nazis' (Crouch 1987: 205). Comparisons between slavery and the Holocaust find a common focus not, as Crouch suggests, in any misguided attempt to establish a quantitative hierarchy of suffering, but in a critical awareness of the inevitably ambivalent status that Enlightenment rationality, with its rhetoric of emancipation and accommodation of systematic suffering, must hold for its various victims. In *Beloved*, the figure of Schoolteacher indicates the complicity of the instrumental, objectifying modes of Enlightenment rationality with acts of oppression and control.

Beloved, we learn, has two dreams, 'exploding, and being swallowed' (Morrison 1997: 157), which correspond to the fear of slavery being actively forgotten or simply being swallowed up into the past without an appropriate effort of memory. If anxiety over her lack of corporeal integrity, her body being dismembered or broken into parts, signifies slavery being disremembered, 'being swallowed' suggests the threat posed by temporality to memory and meaning. The memory of North American slavery that Beloved represents cannot be 'passed on' in the sense of overlooked and neglected, or else it may be 'passed on' in the sense that its structural impact on the present be ignored. *Beloved* would seem here to strike a different note to *The Human Stain*, with the latter's reflection that 'Nothing lasts, and yet nothing passes, either. And nothing passes just because nothing lasts' (Roth 2001: 52). The nearest danger for Morrison is that without a conscious effort of individual and collective will, the memory of slavery will pass into oblivion; the haunting in *Beloved* conveys the worry that the US will *cease* to be haunted.

Beloved herself occupies an interesting position here. To simplify, it would be logical to assume that her 'fully realized presence' at 124 corresponds to the fundamentally positive remembering of slavery. In fact Sethe's 'click', her realization (or decision) that Beloved is her daughter, provokes a different kind of relief, 'smiling, smiling at the things she would not have to remember now' (Morrison 1997: 214), in which Sethe enters into a 'no-time' (225). Beloved's final exorcism or banishment, then, becomes both a victory and a defeat and, as such, a call to cultural memory or, to use one of the novel's key terms, a laying down of narrative tracks 'out there, in the world' (43). As the narrator says of Denver, 'Easily she stepped into the told story that lay before her eyes on the path she followed away from the window' (36). *Beloved* similarly aims to give voice to (or hear) the slave experience, fashioning a told story or path. Sethe's arresting prayer/meditation on temporality can also be read in these terms:

I was talking about time. It's so hard for me to believe in it. Some things go. Pass on. Some things just stay. I used to think it was my rememory. You know. Some things you forget. Other things you never do. But it's not. Places, places are still there. If a house burns down, it's gone, but the place – the picture of it – stays, and not just in my rememory, but out there, in the world. What I remember is a picture floating around out there outside my head. I mean, even if I don't think it, even if I die, the picture of what I did, or knew, or saw is still out there. Right in the place where it happened. (43)

In part, Sethe's speech expresses her fear that time is static, that horrific events simply won't pass; these are the words of a Sethe still preoccupied with the daily 'work of beating back the past'. It may also be read however as in some sense a fantasy on Morrison's part of historical legibility – locating memory spatially and inter-subjectively as a way to overcome the obliteration of memory and meaning threatened by time. In this sense *Beloved* confirms Zuckerman's description of the novelist's characteristic activity as 'entering into professional competition with death' (Roth 2000: 338).

See it, if you can, as history

No less than *Beloved*, *The Human Stain* is self-consciously concerned with national identity. This novel, the final part of Roth's 'American Trilogy', narrated by his fictional alter ego, Nathan Zuckerman, explores key periods in contemporary US history. Thematically, Roth's trilogy explores history's unpredictable but decisive tendency to intrude upon and up-end the seemingly autonomous, seemingly private lives of individuals, along with the opacity of individuals and the illusory nature of our claims to 'know' others at all. The first novel, *American Pastoral* (1997), explores the anti-war protests and counter-cultural upheavals of the 1960s Vietnam era, while the second, *I Married a Communist* (1998), explores the anti-communist McCarthyism of the late 1940s.

Which historical period does *The Human Stain* foreground? Roth has described finishing the two earlier novels and considering new historical material for *The Human Stain*:

I thought, what else do you know? And I said for god sakes, it's right in front of you, it's right in front of your nose. And there it was, of course. And I thought, treat '98 as though it were '48, treat '98 as though it were '68. You see? See it, if you can, as history. (cited in Royal 2006: 114)

The principal event that *The Human Stain* tries to 'see as history' is the impeachment of Bill Clinton following revelations of his White House indiscretions with a young intern, Monica Lewinsky. Opening in the summer of 1998 when Clinton's secret 'emerged in every last mortifying detail – every last *lifelike* detail' (Roth 2001: 2), *The Human Stain* closes in 1999 'on the first February Sunday after the Senate had voted not to remove Bill Clinton from office' (344). Zuckerman is notably tolerant of Clinton's indiscretions, however, which he takes to exemplify an all too human fallibility. His narrative interest lies elsewhere, in the opportunistic moralizing of Clinton's political opponents: the 'enormous piety binge, a purity binge' (2) surrounding their attempt to impeach the president. In a novel of masquerades – 'of exposing and concealing at the same time' (345) – their 'calculated frenzy' (2) masks political interest as moral virtue: a fine distinction when contemporary US political struggles have often taken the form of a war over cultural values.

The sanctimony surrounding Clinton's impeachment provides the affective backdrop for a parallel fictional scandal involving Coleman Silk, a professor of classics. In his late sixties, Coleman returns to the classroom to 'round out his career' after a decade and a half as a 'steamrolling' dean of faculty (5). Exasperated by the failure of two students to attend classes, Coleman asks the seminar, '"Does anybody know these people? Do they exist or are they spooks?"' (7). Coleman has never seen the pair and is unaware that they are African American. Since 'spook' is a derogatory, if antiquated term for African Americans, however, the two students take offence when they learn of his remark. The university takes the complaint seriously, leading to a charge of racism that, for Coleman, is spurious – not so much false as absurd. In the ensuing controversy and struggle to defend his reputation, Coleman's anger turns to rage when his wife Iris dies of a stroke – a direct result he believes of the considerable strain of fighting his corner. Although Coleman resigns in protest rather than disgrace, the local newspaper headline – 'Ex-Dean Leaves College under Racist Cloud' (76) – threatens to have the last word.

Coleman begins a relationship with Faunia Farley, a woman half his age who works as a janitor at Athena College. Their relationship, which parallels Clinton's affair with Lewinsky, subjects him to the censoriousness of his family and former colleagues who consider their involvement inappropriate. Coleman and Faunia die in a car crash, and Zuckerman becomes convinced that Faunia's ex-husband, Vietnam veteran Lester Farley, has driven the two off the road in a jealous rage.

The 'spooks' incident allows Roth to satirize another of the novel's key contemporary contexts, the academic or 'cultural' left, cast in an unflattering light as 'a well-mannered gang of elitist egalitarians who hide their ambition behind high-minded ideals' (80). The political correctness of the academy is compared to McCarthyism ('98 seen as '48), with the charge of racism against Coleman at best exploited as 'an organizing issue' (17) and at worst, malicious. The accusation that Coleman is racist is further complicated – to put it mildly – by the narrator's discovery at Coleman's funeral that his friend was a light-skinned African American 'passing' as Jewish throughout his marriage and academic career. Surmising that Coleman's affair with Faunia was regenerative because he told her his secret, Zuckerman marvels at his 'utterly transformed friend' (338). If the 'transformation' in question is ambiguous between Coleman's death and exposed identity, it also anticipates the imaginative reconstruction that Zuckerman's account of his friend's life will necessarily involve.

Rage

A 'state of the nation' novel, *The Human Stain* suggests that if anything unifies the bitterly disunited 'Age of Clinton', it is rage. A 'corroding indignation' (63), corrosive of self and society, rage becomes an organizing concern in *The Human Stain*. Framing his predicament in terms drawn from classical literature, Coleman is implicitly cast by Zuckerman as a latter-day Achilles, 'highly flammable [...] alienated and estranged by a slight to his honor' (5). Elsewhere, Coleman's very fate is decided by Lester Farley's rage. Farley's failure to attain catharsis through a visit to the moving wall Vietnam memorial (256) leads, Zuckerman's narrative suggests, to the murder of Faunia and 'her enraging lover' Coleman (294). While 'it doesn't take much to put him into a rage' (66) Farley is not alone here. Delphine Roux, Coleman's academic colleague, is 'unable to contain her outrage' (195) after learning of his affair with Faunia. Coleman's brother Walt, meanwhile, 'was always a little angrier about everything' (104) and considers his brother's passing an 'outrage' (336).

Appropriately for a novel set in a period when 'both sides wondered "Why are we so crazy?"' (3), rage seems to be the only thing that the novel's characters have in common. Farley becomes the representative character, signposting the direction in which the rest of the novel's population seems headed, hence Zuckerman's comment to Farley: 'I write about people like you' (356). While Farley resembles the perfect stereotype of the disaffected and traumatized Vietnam veteran – that stock character of recent US fiction and film – his monomaniac presence should invoke the Oklahoma City bomber Timothy McVeigh rather than *Taxi Driver*'s Travis Bickle. By taking Farley's subjectivity as representative, *The Human Stain* identifies the loss of a capacity at once political and novelistic, the stereotypically liberal, empathic ability to transcend one's own subject position as a condition of community.

If Zuckerman's telling of Coleman's story necessarily involves imaginative transformation, Zuckerman is relatively frank about the gaps in his knowledge. He merely assumes, for example, that Farley murdered Coleman and Faunia. Neither does he know that Delphine sent the anonymous note to Coleman, and, assuming she did, he cannot know the circumstances and motivation of her action. The inclusion in Zuckerman's text of conspicuously conscientious passages explaining how he knows as much as he does distracts attention from the novel's significant shifts in narrative perspective. A key gap in knowledge that Zuckerman's narrative undertakes to fill imaginatively concerns Coleman's 'passing'. Zuckerman only learns of his friend's origins at his funeral and, although he gathers details from Ernestine and (possibly) Walt, key passages of *The Human Stain* focalized from Coleman's perspective drastically exceed the scope of Zuckerman's knowledge.

Zuckerman's response to such gaps and uncertainties is to remind us that, in life no less than in fiction, what passes for knowledge of others is to a significant extent imagined, so that his novelistic activity of imputing human motive is no different in kind from the way that we cohere our 'knowledge' of others off the page. This uncertainty is well illustrated, for Zuckerman, by the revelation of Coleman's hidden origins. Such reminders of the ineradicable precariousness of our claims to knowledge, moreover, can have a redemptive and democratizing effect on the polarized, fixated and enraged subjectivities in *The Human Stain*, which are premised on misplaced certainties. More than the 'Whodunit?' (356) Farley expects, then, Zuckerman's book provides a cultural diagnosis. His confessedly fictional speculations as to Delphine and Coleman's actions and subjectivities are meant to secure a broad narrative moral rather than to establish the absolute verisimilitude of his account. (What else should we expect from 'that great opportunistic maw, a novelist's mind'? (170)) By styling Delphine, for example, as unaware of her true motivation for sending the note – her infatuation with Coleman who she believes is infatuated with her – Zuckerman has her illustrate his novel's insight that, despite the title of her note, nobody *knows*.

The Human Stain argues that, although polarized, the left and right have in common a sanctimony resembling the propriety by which Coleman considers himself tyrannized. Such moralizing implies a damaging appeal to an impossible purity. The most destructive human stain of all involves the denial of human imperfection and the invocation of a disfiguring fantasy of stainlessness, 'for what is the insistence on purity if not *more* impurity?' (242). Roth has Zuckerman align this central narrative moral with Faunia – who he barely met, of course – casting her as reconciled to imperfection so that hers is a rage 'without the rage' (29), although such privileged, saving knowledge hardly makes her less of a one-dimensional character.

Zuckerman's book forms an intervention into a US culture that has lost its appetite and inclination for a hermeneutics of suspicion and complexity and is, as such, post-novelistic:

> It's not as though Marx or Freud or Darwin or Stalin or Hitler or Mao had never happened, it's as though Sinclair Lewis had not happened. It's, he thought, as though *Babbitt* had never been written. It's as though not even that most basic level of imaginative thought had been admitted into consciousness to cause the slightest disturbance. (153)

Along with the novel's 'chorus' of men discussing Monica Lewinsky as embodying a 'generation that is proud of its shallowness', whose 'whole language is a summation of the stupidity of the last forty years' (147), such passages are indicative of the novel's textual norms. The corrosive, riotous laughter in *The Human Stain* complicates any critical attempt to ascertain a stable hierarchy of voices in the text. Like Coleman, Roth's novel privileges a 'sliding relationship with things' (208). Roth, Zuckerman and Coleman share a specific sensibility nonetheless. Although Zuckerman refuses to exempt himself from his novel's critique of purity by returning to the social and having his book join 'the jumble, the mayhem, the mess' (3), a hierarchical relationship is implied here, since that return consists in confronting the culture with a complex object.

Springing the historical lock

Zuckerman's narrative is minded to trouble pious certainties by dramatizing the moral, psychological and historical complexities of his main protagonist, 'more subtle than this one's ideology and that one's morality' (3). Is Coleman's passing the villainous act of race betrayal that we might expect from Coleman *Brutus* Silk, or a heroic and ideologically American act of self-fashioning? Both responses are rehearsed in *The Human Stain*, discursively through Zuckerman's extensive meditations on passing, and dramatically through Coleman's 'harshly ironic fate' (333). Zuckerman discourages us from taking an easy position on Coleman's 'deceptions' by insisting on 'the indivisibility of the heroism and the disgrace' (184). Before considering Coleman's passing in those terms, we should note that Zuckerman's adoption of Coleman's perspective might be seen as a further instance of passing, since it involves a Jewish American narrator assuming the persona of his African American protagonist (a protagonist who is in turn passing as Jewish American). Passing begins to resemble the novelist's activity as such – predicated on the universalist assumption of our common intelligibility to one another – although justified and called for by the recognition that 'our understanding of people must always be at best slightly wrong' (22). While Zuckerman's telling of Coleman's story stages various comparisons between passing and writing, the comparisons work in both directions: writing also resembles passing.

The 'heroism' attaching to Coleman's passing consists in the uncompromising effort of will with which he undertakes to pioneer 'the I' (108). It is worth recalling here that, as portrayed by Zuckerman, Coleman's decision to pass is not entirely undertaken for the logical and instrumental reason of 'slipping the punch' of racism. Coleman also passes for the exhilarating, problematic secrecy. With the birth of their four children, whose skin pigmentation does not reveal his background, a relieved and emotional Coleman decides to tell Iris his secret. After Iris condemns a friend's husband for keeping a similarly drastic secret from his wife, however, Coleman realizes that he cannot reveal his origins and rebukes himself for the sentimental wavering of his resolve:

> As though the battle that is each person's singular battle could somehow be abjured, as though voluntarily one could pick up and leave off being one's self, the characteristic immutable self in whose behalf the battle is taken in the first place. (179)

At first glance this appears a paradoxical formulation: a reminder to be true to oneself by continuing to pose as someone else? Hasn't Coleman precisely picked up and left off being himself? The 'characteristic self' here, however, is not the socially inscribed racial self but a prior self – 'the raw I' (108) – to which Coleman remains true, or which Zuckerman's narrative privileges.

So although Zuckerman responds with hostility when Herb Keble, the African American political scientist persuaded to give Coleman's funeral oration, belatedly praises his once-shunned colleague as 'an American individualist *par excellence*', Zuckerman's issue is with Keble's sincerity rather than the appropriateness of the comparison. If framing Coleman's passing in terms of fidelity to a pre-racial 'characteristic' self denaturalizes racial being, it also invokes the rootless self of individualism, allowing Roth to familiarize passing by casting it in national terms: 'Was he merely being another American and, in the great frontier tradition, accepting the democratic invitation to throw your origins overboard if to do so contributes to the pursuit of happiness?' (334). Keble is unaware of just how right he is, and his comments suggest an unwitting critique of individualism: see what happens to the American individualist.

Coleman's passing is as much an attempt to evade hierarchies of class as of race, hierarchies shown in the novel to be inter-articulated. His father forbids him from training 'at the Newark Boys Club, which to Mr. Silk was for slum kids, for illiterates and hoodlums bound for either the gutter or jail' and has him train instead under Doc Chizner with 'privileged Jewish kids' in East Orange (97). It is Chizner who first suggests that Coleman might pass for white, confirming in an unexpected way Mr. Silk's conviction that Jewish

American assimilation might provide a model for African American upward social mobility: 'the Jews [...] were like Indian scouts, shrewd people showing the outsider his way in, showing the social possibility, showing an intelligent colored family how it might be done' (97). When Coleman enters Howard University 'with the privileged children of the black professional elite', class differences emerge: 'he began to think that there was something of the nigger about him even to the kids in his dorm who had all sorts of new clothes and money in their pockets' (106). Such intra-racial class distinctions become less salient, however, in the broader social context: 'In the segregated South there were no separate identities, not even for him and his roommate. No such subtleties allowed, and the impact was devastating' (103).

Coleman's passing becomes a response to the social phenomenon of 'forced grouping' in which individual differences, however pronounced, become less salient than membership of a racially defined group. His passing may be seen as an assertion of individuality rather than of individualism: 'Never for him the tyranny of the we that is dying to suck you in, the coercive, inclusive, historical, inescapable moral *we* with its insidious *E pluribus unum*' (208). At low ebb, Coleman imagines his father rebuking him by sardonically referring to the son's 'passionate struggle for precious singularity, his revolt of one against the Negro fate' (183). And yet Coleman's father, we learn, also tried to refashion himself, quitting Southern agricultural college and moving north in the Great Migration to African American modernity. Although the father's business fails with the Depression, he was no less willing than the son to cast off the regulatory fictions of race and make up his own story.

The argument that Coleman's passing constitutes an act of betrayal is voiced by Walt, whose opinions we learn through Ernestine. Walt despises Coleman for disowning their mother and because there was a struggle to fight in post-war, pre-civil-rights era America, and, by passing, Coleman avoided that struggle. As Ernestine notes, 'I think he was insulted and flared up – not just for Mother but for all of us. Walt was the political member of the family' (319). Ernestine is one of the heroes of *The Human Stain* for her ability to transcend anger with a rational, mediating voice. One of her attempts to placate Walt's outrage, a response that she 'only half' believes, is resonant:

> Coleman was a part of his time, I tell him. Coleman couldn't wait to go through civil rights to get to his human rights, and so he skipped a step. 'See him historically,' I say to Walt. 'You're a history teacher – see him as something larger.' (327)

The problem here is that 'skipping a step' implies civil rights were historically inevitable, would come automatically with time. Martin Luther King described this assumption as 'a tragic misconception [...] the strangely irrational notion that there is something in the very flow of time that will inevitably cure all ills' (King 2000: 74). King's target here, though, is the white liberal, and surely Coleman shared King's impatience – why should he wait?

Still reeling from the discovery of his friend's secret, Zuckerman takes up Ernestine's suggestion of thinking Coleman historically:

> The man who decides to forge a distinct historical destiny, who sets out to spring the historical lock, and who does so, brilliantly succeeds at altering his personal lot, only to be ensnared by the history that he hadn't quite counted on: the history that isn't yet history, the history that the clock is now ticking off, the history proliferating as I write, accruing a minute at a time and grasped better by the future than it will ever be by us. The we that is inescapable: the present moment, the common lot, the current mood, the mind of one's country, the stranglehold of history that is one's own time. Blindsided by the terrifyingly provisional nature of everything. (Roth 2001: 335)

Zuckerman's reflections remind us of something easy to overlook in *The Human Stain*. Coleman doesn't come to grief through the exposure of his secret or through the past catching up with him, even if that is how it feels, to us and to him. Far from it – although Coleman is cynically 'exposed' as a supposed racist, his ascribed racial identity remains undisclosed until, we are led to imagine, the eventual publication of Zuckerman's book. Coleman is able to escape his past, but is undone by the 'current mood' of 1998 or 'the stranglehold of history that is one's own time', a stranglehold of propriety that Zuckerman's text seeks to loosen.

Specifically, Coleman falls foul of a US academy of the late 1990s dominated by the proprieties of the cultural left, with its signature interest in identity politics and questions of representation. The significance of passing in *The Human Stain* is complicated in interesting ways by the novel's campus setting. Put simply, identity politics abandoned earlier liberal attempts to overcome 'the great American menace' (106) of racism by arguing for a 'colour blind' world in which race wouldn't matter, and sought instead to combat racism by inverting the negative evaluations surrounding racial difference. According to the logic of identity politics, the way to overcome racism was to celebrate rather than ignore racial difference and ethnic diversity, uncovering the hidden histories that had been repressed through conforming US national identity to a hegemonic and dominant WASP (White Anglo-Saxon Protestant) narrative.

Locating passing in the midst of identity politics makes for some unexpected implications. We might assume that passing, seen through the lens of identity politics, is both an anachronism and a betrayal. Coleman entirely avoids the cultural-political imperative of representing his African American identity and therefore comes to grief in identifying with a white norm that is a regulatory fiction of power rather than a stable and democratically available subject position. And yet one of the most striking implications of *The Human Stain* is that passing, while certainly anachronistic, is also suggestive of a theoretically sophisticated attitude to identity. Might not passing be seen as a theoretical advance on, or at least a corrective to, identity politics in its troubling of the static and prescriptive assumptions about identity that identity politics might be understood to require? The philosopher Anthony Appiah has argued, for example, that 'if we are to move beyond racism we shall have, in the end, to move beyond current racial identities' (1996: 55), so that Coleman's refusal to 'allow his prospects to be unjustly limited by so arbitrary a classification as race' (Roth 2001: 20) might be thought to situate him in the theoretical avant-garde.

On this reading, passing puts pressure on the very idea of fixed categories of racial identity by foregrounding the uniformity with which the multivalent spectrum of human skin pigmentation – the human stain – gets reductively classified in terms of the binary logic of 'black' or 'white'. We might recall here the linguistic precision Coleman's father instilled in his children, who 'learned things had classifications. They learned the power of naming precisely' (93). Historically, however, in a US context, the power of naming racial identity 'precisely' has had less to do with precision in the sense of accurate description than with the repetition and maintenance of brutal legal, social and cultural hierarchies and exclusions. Appropriately, then, racial difference in *The Human Stain* is often hard to describe in precise terms. Zuckerman's initial description of Coleman's appearance, although noting his 'ambiguous aura', works conspicuously hard to conform his friend's identity to a classifiable ethno-racial 'type' by accommodating exceptions to the stereotypical rule, 'the small-nosed Jewish type with the facial heft in the jaw, one of those crimped-haired Jews of a light yellowish skin pigmentation' (17). When Zuckerman meets Ernestine, it is only the incorrect assumption that she is Keble's wife that leads him to add 'one clue to another to matter-of-factly register her as black' (316). So although Zuckerman is right about Ernestine, he isn't able to 'tell' from her appearance alone, recalling Steena's love note: 'How much can I tell / of what I see in him?' (112)

If *The Human Stain* 'spooks' identity politics by working to denaturalize racial classifications, this is nowhere more evident than in the 'spooks' incident itself. Zuckerman imagines an exasperated Coleman reminding a committee, 'But how could I know they were black students if I had never laid eyes on them and, other than their names, had no knowledge of them?' (85). Coleman, of course, *is* visible to his accusers, who still do not 'know' that he 'is' black. The implication here is that the essentialist logic of racial difference as fixed and knowable overrides the empirical visible fact of similarity – a sure sign of ideology. Essentialist notions of race are reduced to absurdity in Coleman's paranoid misreading of Steena's note: '*I see clear through to the back of your negro*' (113).

Passing might be taken to imply a fluid approach to identity and to demonstrate the fictions of race, then, but only by exposing the degree to which such utopian fluidity or post-racial consciousness is absolutely forbidden. Forbidden, moreover, no less by the essentialist premise of identity politics than by the racist reliance on knowable and fixed racial demarcations. The spooks incident finds Coleman able to escape his past but unable to escape a category. Coleman escapes the racism that insists on fixed and delimiting identities, only to be undone by an anti-racism that similarly privileges being over becoming. The association of passing with fluidity is further complicated if we remember something that is symptomatically easy to overlook in *The Human Stain*. Coleman is a light-skinned African American passing, after his marriage to Iris, not as white but as an assimilated Jew, prompting Zuckerman's description of

Coleman as 'a heretofore unknown amalgam of the most unalike of America's historical undesirables' (132). Although Zuckerman regularly describes Coleman passing as 'white', this is true only in the sense that he wants to claim for himself the cultural privileges of 'whiteness': its passing *itself* off, not as a further and salient ethnoracial identity, but as a neutral norm.

This returns us to Zuckerman's description of Coleman as springing 'the historical lock'. Most obviously, to spring the historical lock is to transcend history by freeing oneself from its confines. This is, of course, hubris. Viewing Coleman's predicament through the lens of classical literature, as Zuckerman does in *The Human Stain*, inevitably alters its significance. The problem for Coleman becomes not passing so much as the misguided assumption of individual potency implied by his attempt to cohere and shape the self against a chaotic, unstable and meaningless outer world. His attempt at self-fashioning becomes heroic and universal – continuous with self-formation as such.

Such a universal perspective, stressing the metaphysical impossibility of self-fashioning, obscures the specific historical character of Coleman's passing. Coleman attempts a task that is socially rather than metaphysically impossible – to outrun the categories of race in a society that insists on their presence ('how accidentally a destiny is made' (125)). If framing his predicament in terms of 'the history of the human race over the last three thousand years' (240) enables a salutary reminder of our invariant impurity and volatility, it also risks obscuring the genuine possibility of progressive social change in the present: the undeniable social and political changes undertaken, for example, in the civil rights movement as participated in by Walt, or the important work undertaken by the cultural left as represented by Delphine Roux. On this reading, it would be premature to universalize Coleman's 'harshly ironic fate' in metaphysical terms. From Walt's perspective, perhaps, Coleman tries to evade history and so becomes its victim rather than an agent. In another sense, then, to spring the historical lock would involve entering into history rather than escaping it – understanding the present historically through agency. Picking the historical lock in this sense is something that Coleman doesn't do because, in Walt's understanding, this would entail entering into the present by participating in its struggles. It should be noted however that despite their estrangement, Walt is closer to Coleman than he is to identity politics in the logic of Roth's novel, because his argument for civil rights is predicated on a universal vision rather than on an assertion of difference. As Ernestine puts it: 'It's *because* he's a human being that he believes that what you do, you do to advance the race' (327).

This brings us to the question of how we should read the fact that the novel's traditionalist defender of the canon is African American. There are ironies here both to relish and to despair of. Coleman feels, for example, that the spooks incident is exploited to secure further 'representation' in the sense of recruitment of African American faculty; Coleman's passing means that he simultaneously does and does not 'represent' African Americans in that sense. For Zuckerman, Coleman becomes heroic to the extent that he refuses to have his identity dictated by the putative responsibility to represent 'his' group. Entangling Coleman in a complex and contradictory web of hermeneutic frames, *The Human Stain* uses the spooks incident to put destabilizing pressure on identity politics and its potentially limiting assumptions. The tragedy here is that Coleman insists on living as if race does not matter in a culture that absolutely refuses to let race pass.

If pioneering the 'I' wins Coleman some distance from forced grouping – sidestepping the regulatory fictions of race through the counter-move of fictionalizing his own identity – it also leaves him stranded. The very identity politics and efforts to broaden and politicize the canon that appear reduced in *The Human Stain* to unthinking pieties would offer Coleman a useful resource for contesting the social tragedy or 'American menace' of racism. The issue for Roth is that such attempts to overcome racism nevertheless reintroduce a sense in which race becomes fate. If *Beloved* mobilizes the framework of identity politics to pass on a story that would otherwise be passed by, *The Human Stain* tells a story that troubles that framework but also attests to its necessity and value.

CHAPTER FIVE

THE CONTEMPORARY AMERICAS NOVEL

BLOOD MERIDIAN (1985), *ALMANAC OF THE DEAD* (1991), *THE BRIEF WONDROUS LIFE OF OSCAR WAO* (2007)

From nation to hemisphere

American, as it appears in the title of this book, may seem a straight-forward and uncontroversial marker of place, an adjective fitting the United States like a glove. From Bret Easton Ellis's *American Psycho* (1991) to Green Day's *American Idiot* (2004), cultural production in the US continues to take the word as referring unproblematically to the nation composed of the forty-eight contiguous states lying between Canada and Mexico, together with Alaska and Hawaii. For all its familiarity, however, this terminological manoeuvre is suspect and should be resisted. Jan Radway famously makes the case for dissent in 'What's in a Name?', arguing that 'to elide the idea of the American with the culture of the United States' is to overlook, or wilfully suppress, 'the fact that other nations, groups, and territories had already staked their own quite distinctive claim to the concept and name American' (2002: 49). The rights of the US to exclusive ownership of the term *American* should, Radway says, be contested and the word's field of reference considerably enlarged so as to include also 'the America of those who claimed South and Central America, the America of the Caribbean basin, as their home' (49). To pretend otherwise, to continue to conflate *American* with the United States, is no mere academic matter but actually an 'imperial gesture' (50).

Published between 1985 and 2007, the three novels that are our focus in this chapter offer precisely the kind of expansive under-standing of America for which Radway and many others have recently argued. The products of writers who carry United States passports, they trace nevertheless complex geographies in which the US is no longer centrally placed but sited in larger constellations of the Americas. These texts, then, adjust their scale from the nation to the hemisphere, venturing into representation of neighbouring states in Central and South America and in the Caribbean. The 'hemispheric turn' manifested here is perhaps the most important of several *transnational* developments in the recent fiction of the United States (a topic explored further in Chapter 6). This is not to say, of course, that writers of the US before our period took no interest in their country's neighbours. Among earlier texts engaged to a greater or lesser extent with Mexico, for example, is Jack Kerouac's *On the Road* (1957), high-water mark of the Beat movement and a novel in which movement south from the United States carries for the protagonists the possibility of spiritual and erotic liberation. Without discounting the importance of such precursors, however, there is in the group of contemporary texts with which this chapter is concerned an enhanced geographical consciousness, a deliberate attempt at remapping that connects the nation to its region along lines of power and desire. Only such outward-looking fiction, it is felt, can generate adequate under-standing of the United States itself. As Junot Díaz, one of the three novelists discussed here, puts it: 'You can't talk about the United States unless your first words are "Santo Domingo." That's just the way it works' (Celayo and Shook 2008: 16).

In 1493 Santo Domingo in the Dominican Republic (formerly Dominica), later to be the birthplace of Junot Díaz, was a point of disembarkation for Christopher Columbus during his imperial voyage to the Americas. From this part of the Caribbean, white conquest extended across the region, including into the territory that would become the United States. As we will show, Díaz's novel, *The Brief Wondrous Life of Oscar Wao* (2007) teases out modern entanglements of the US and the Dominican Republic, taking the relationship between these two nations as symptomatic of the 'cognitive instability and asymmetrical power' that one theorist says characterize cross-border dynamics in the contemporary Americas (Siemerling 2005: 6). In a notably complex temporal structure, the novel moves forwards through the title character's experiences of disorientation and romantic yearning in both New Jersey and the Dominican Republic, but also backwards through successive generations of his family's history in the politically repressive DR.

The chapter's other two texts have different geographical foci, but share *Oscar Wao*'s commitment to hemispheric representation. *Blood Meridian: Or, The Evening Redness in the West* (1985), by Cormac McCarthy, returns to the middle of the nineteenth century, narrating one of the earliest, and bloodiest, episodes of frontier-crossing between the United States and Mexico: the depredations carried out in the Mexican states of Chihuahua and Sonora in 1849 by a gang of American mercenaries, hired, under the leadership of Captain Glanton and Judge Holden, to protect Chihuahuan land from incursions by Indian raiders. In *Almanac of the Dead* (1991), the Native American writer Leslie Marmon Silko ranges further still in the Americas, moving outwards from her Laguna Pueblo community in New Mexico to explore not only the complex political and cultural enclaves of the US/Mexico borderlands, but also other hemispheric sites including Colombia and Haiti. Her large-scale narrative describes a transnational and transgenerational struggle between those who would exploit and asset-strip the Americas (mining conglomerates, resort developers, imperialists and neo-imperialists of every kind), and those, notably Mexicans and Native Americans mobilizing both traditional models of ecological sensitivity and newer vocabularies of political liberation, who seek its deliverance. By juxtaposing these three texts, we hope to give an adequate account of one of the most significant strains in current United States fiction. Nevertheless, we do not seek to identify a single aesthetics and a single politics. Rather, the chapter aims to register and evaluate the formal and stylistic variety, the historical and geographical differences, and the ideological pluralism of the contemporary Americas novel.

'Alternative trails, or other maneuvers'

Blood Meridian, Almanac of the Dead and *The Brief Wondrous Life of Oscar Wao* are bound together thematically, but are very divergent formally. In thinking about form in these novels, it is advisable to follow the practice of José David Saldívar, one of the foremost contemporary theorists of 'the border'. Saldívar notes that his own exploration of cultural work produced by writers, artists and musicians along the US/Mexico line is not intended 'to codify' what he calls 'border discourse', nor is it aiming 'to unify a rhetoric or stylistics of the border' (1997: 14). The three border novels discussed in this chapter are not only rhetorically and stylistically different from one another: each is internally heterogeneous, too, generating a reading experience that is jagged rather than smooth or singular. To reckon with the enduring complications of the Americas, the texts pursue multiple literary trajectories; they seek, at the level of form itself, what one of Silko's characters in *Almanac of the Dead*, looking for the best routes through the Arizona/Mexico borderlands, calls 'alternative trails, or other maneuvers' (1992: 220).

The evidence of these texts suggests, for example, that the contemporary Americas novel traverses many genres. Díaz, McCarthy and Silko, it seems, share a sensibility with the young Oscar Wao himself, who is described as taking an unusually strong interest 'in Genres!' (Díaz 2008: 17). *The Brief Wondrous Life of Oscar Wao* itself is multiply, even chaotically, 'genred'. Partly a mock-scholarly history of the Dominican Republic (fulfilling this task in playful footnotes as well as in the narrative proper), the novel is also postcolonial polemic, black comedy, *Bildungsroman*, improbable love story and family saga. Its leavening of political urgencies with the familiar pleasures of, say, the family saga is evidence, along with similar generic mixing in fictions like Jonathan Franzen's *The Corrections* (2001) and *Freedom* (2010), of what Benjamin Kunkel calls 'the literary populism that we can now recognize as one of the main trends of the American novel over the past decade or so' (2010: 13). Yet *Oscar Wao* also positions itself among genres that mobilize subcultural, rather than mass, readerships. In both its repertoire of allusions and, more substantially, in how it stages the strange, disorienting transits characters make between rural Dominican Republic and metropolitan New York, the novel ventures beyond realist options and into the genres of science fiction and fantasy. Non- or even anti-realistic is, of course, not synonymous here with non- or anti-political. Díaz retools for serious ideological purpose genres that might seem degraded or, in the text's own terms, the preserve of 'nerdboys' (2008: 23). As he says in interview, SF's foregrounding of themes of voyaging and being out of place, its interest in modelling other worlds, make such a genre particularly well-suited to frame 'the history of the immigrant, the minority, the woman' (Celayo and Shook 2008: 15).

By comparison with Díaz's crowd-pleasing effects in *Oscar Wao*, many of Silko's strategies in *Almanac of the Dead* seem designed to negate any possibility of general readership. There is, to begin with, the novel's monumental scale: reaching to 763 pages, and with multiple plot strands involving more than fifty characters, it is, in Silko's own words, 'long and complex to the point of being foolhardy' (cited in Roppolo 2007: 544). Then, similarly inhibiting the emergence of a large, consensual audience, there is the ferocity of its tone. From as early as words written on the 'five hundred year map' that is included in the novel before storytelling begins, *Almanac of the Dead* identifies itself as an Indian revenge fantasy: 'The Indian Wars have never ended in the Americas. Native Americans acknowledge no borders; they seek nothing less than the return of tribal lands' (Silko 1992: 15). And yet, for all these intransigent qualities, Silko's text is not without some populist appeal of its own. As the multi-stranded plot unravels in the US/Mexico borderlands and beyond, there are resemblances to the kind of highly mobile political thriller familiar from the recent cinema of the United States as well as from its literature (the novels comprising the Bourne Trilogy (1980–90), written by Robert Ludlum and all subsequently filmed, would be pertinent examples). For the reader, enjoyable generic payoffs accompany, as in *Oscar Wao*, the reception of a militant politics.

To some extent, however, *Almanac of the Dead* also breaks free from the system of genres which has been validated by literary criticism in Europe and the United States. Legible enough as conspiracy thriller and anti-colonial polemic, it positions itself too among specifically Native American forms of verbal production, including tribal prayer and folkloric narrative. Most crucially, it borrows from the form of the *codex*, a repository of communal knowledge of religion, cosmology, medicine and history especially associated with the Aztec, Mixtec and Mayan peoples of Central America. While, historically, there were three Mayan codices, the novel's plot turns around the identification of a fourth which predicts the eventual disappearance of Europeans from the Americas and which, piece by piece, is being reassembled by various characters. Yet Silko's text is not simply about a codex, or almanac, of this sort; as Shari M. Huhndorf points out, it 'in fact itself resembles a codex' (2009: 160). *Almanac of the Dead*'s utilization of categories of Native expression thus goes some way towards 'indigenizing' the genre set of the contemporary United States novel itself.

Just as Silko's oscillations between contemporary political thriller and traditional tribal narrative have an unsettling effect upon the reader, so too a sense of disorientation is produced by McCarthy's behaviour towards genres in *Blood Meridian*. Barcley Owens writes of how generic plurality here deflects any simple encoding of the novel: 'Is McCarthy spinning an adventure story, a tall tale, tragedy, horror, historical romance, dark comedy, revisionist fiction or some kind of postmodern experiment?' (2000: 16). Oddly, Owens does not include the western in this list. Structured for the most part by the itinerary of violent nineteenth-century Americans marauding across arid Western landscapes made familiar by dime novels and John Wayne films, *Blood Meridian* traces on every page the popular western's signatures. Yet even as McCarthy meets expectations (by, for instance, supplying scenes of physical violence), he does so with such frequency and excess as to make his novel seem like a self-conscious performing of the western, not so much a 'straight' example of the genre as a fantastical or baroque variation. In addition, kinds of literature that are customarily kept apart criss-cross, appropriately enough, in the geographical borderlands mapped by this text. Here it is significant that *Blood Meridian* marked McCarthy's turn to the West, and to the western, after four previous novels set in rural Tennessee that are usually categorized as examples of 'Southern Gothic'. Rather than being disavowed, however, gothic traces are present in *Blood Meridian* too, lodged in its system like so many foreign bodies. Take, for instance, McCarthy's description of a 'bloodbat', or 'vampire', which is an unexpected night-time visitant to a gravely wounded member of the mercenary gang: 'It leaned to him. It crafted in his neck two narrow grooves and folding its wings over him it began to drink his blood' (1989: 66). With horror of this kind, as well as with black comedy, McCarthy scrambles the codes of the western, raising not only formal but also ideological questions which will be discussed later in this chapter.

Any reading of *Blood Meridian* has to reckon not only with genre but with the complex materiality of McCarthy's prose itself. Questions of style, and its ethics and politics, are posed with particular force by the novel's many descriptions of horrifying violence. What, for example, are the effects on the reader of a moment when Captain Glanton's mercenary gang comes across 'a bush that was hung with dead babies' (57)?

These small victims, seven, eight of them, had holes punched in their underjaws and were hung so by their throats from the broken stobs of a mesquite to stare eyeless at the naked sky. Bald and pale and bloated, larval to some unreckonable being. (57)

From one perspective, McCarthy is here simply fulfilling a revisionist function, violating the convention of bloodlessness in a thousand Hollywood westerns and registering instead the actual scale of barbarism in the Old West. Yet this interpretation risks short-circuiting on contact with the linguistic particulars themselves. For it is not only readers of a worryingly desensitized kind who may be diverted from reflection on these young, terrible casualties into wondering, for example, about the occurrence of the word 'stobs'. Meaning, according to the *Oxford English Dictionary*, 'A stump, portion remaining after mutilation', 'A stick, a twig broken off' and 'A thorn; a prickle; a splinter', the word has a striking, almost flamboyant archaism: indeed, the *OED*'s citations of its use in other texts begin as early as 1420 but extend no nearer our own time than 1851. Simplified moral processing of the scene snags, aptly enough, on the sight and sound of this unexpected lexical object, 'stobs' also exemplifying McCarthy's deployment throughout the novel of an amazingly extensive and obscure vocabulary (from 'halms', 'duledge' and 'gastine' to 'lemniscate', 'holothurians' and 'pampooties').

As well as by lexical play, the reader of the passage just quoted may be unsettled by idiosyncrasy of image and syntax. There is, for instance, the elaborateness of the metaphor by which these babies' bodies become the larvae produced by 'some unreckonable being'. An analogy might be suggested with Milton's practice in *Paradise Lost* (1674), a major influence upon the rhetorical and imagistic procedures of *Blood Meridian*. In Book I, lines 300–2 of his poem, Milton describes the bodies of Satan's fallen angels lying 'Thick as Autumnal Leaves that strow the Brooks / In *Vallombrosa*' (1980: 165). What appeared to be a straightforward description of moral degeneracy is suddenly complicated by Milton's epic simile, with its picturesque detail of fallen leaves. Through his own speculative metaphor, McCarthy, likewise, prompts responses more complex and diverse than those simply of revulsion at the babies' injuries. The reader of the passage may also be drawn, irrelevantly or obtusely as it were, towards noting its syntactic experimentation, in particular its grammatically incomplete closing sentence. Elsewhere in *Blood Meridian*, play with syntax will take less minimalist form, incorporating, for example, sentences that extend to almost a page in length and recall the labyrinthine prose of William Faulkner, the Southern modernist novelist who is another significant influence upon McCarthy's literary practice.

Blood Meridian's conspicuous play with syntax, imagery and lexis might be taken to have an aestheticizing effect. Rather than uncovered and offered for critique in line with what appears to be the novel's official project, the barbaric history of the West is, according to such interpretation, newly burnished by McCarthy. This reading should not be dismissed lightly; nevertheless, politically radical understandings of the text's self-advertising stylistics are also possible. Here it is important to recognize that, like *Almanac of the Dead*, *Blood Meridian* narrates not merely episodes of cross-border imperialist brutality, but, more broadly, the savagery of a developing capitalist economy in the Americas. If McCarthy shows the commodification of violence with the state of Chihuahua paying for each Indian scalp the mercenaries obtain, he evokes, still more disturbingly, the violence of commodification itself. David Holloway notes that, in *Blood Meridian*, the operations of the marketplace reach everywhere, from management of a ferry crossing to trade in buffalo carcases: 'the heterogeneous diversity of the object world is reduced to a single identity, a homogenous mass of matter, a collection of things linked together by their common exchange-value, their shared status as commodities in a commodity world' (2002: 104–5). In this context, McCarthy's foregrounding of style may assume a politically progressive value. Deferring any straightforward processing of the text, these investments in linguistic obscurity, syntactic unorthodoxy and generic inconsistency offer some resistance, potentially, to the reductive tendencies, the processes of uniformity, simplicity and linearity, that, at the level of narrative, *Blood Meridian* shows to be gathering strength in the Americas.

More exuberant than McCarthy, more given to cartoonish, Day-Glo effects, Díaz nevertheless enacts, in *Oscar Wao*, a similar display of literary style itself. The novel is packed with puns and neologisms (as well as with bilingual passages that will be discussed later). Promiscuously, Díaz is liable to wander in the same sentence from colloquialism to formal rhetoric, from allusions to popular song, film and TV to citations of high culture. Here is a description of the emergent sexuality of Belicia, Oscar's mother, when a schoolgirl in the Dominican Republic:

Now fully, ahem, endowed, Beli returned to El Redentor from summer break to the alarm of faculty and students alike and set out to track down Jack Pujols with the great deliberation of Ahab after you-know-who. (And of all these things the albino boy was the symbol. Wonder ye then at the fiery hunt?) (Díaz 2008: 95)

Finding its motivation in the reference to Captain Ahab, 'Wonder ye then at the fiery hunt?' is a direct quotation from Herman Melville's *Moby-Dick* (1851), cornerstone of classic American literature. Yet this sample of canonical writing nestles cheek-by-jowl here with the vernacular contributions of 'ahem' and 'you-know-who'. Along with other classic texts such as Joyce's *Ulysses*, *Moby-Dick* circulates in *Oscar Wao* alongside – rather than above – popular cultural items like the pulp SF of Frank Herbert, the graphic novels of Alan Moore and the music of Bon Jovi.

The eclectic sampling performed by Díaz's novel aligns it with postmodern culture, which Fredric Jameson has described as 'a field of stylistic and discursive heterogeneity without a norm' (1991: 17). In the postmodern moment, cultural artefacts that were previously endowed with high value, even with a kind of priestly authority, have to jostle for space amidst what Jameson evokes as an array of 'masks and voices stored up in the imaginary museum of a now global culture' (18). This is, for Jameson, not something to be unequivocally celebrated, but, on the contrary, a suspicious development, the ready accessibility and exchangeability of multiple styles suggesting the penetration of the law of commodification into the cultural realm, including literature itself. Such a gloomy construction of the postmodern may come to mind, at times, when we consider *Oscar Wao*'s own well-stocked 'supermarket' of verbal resources from lyricism to obscene street-talk, or when we observe that in this novel everything from *Hamlet* to *The Hobbit* seems available for sampling. Yet the politics of postmodernism is multiple rather than singular, contested rather than settled. Just as the conspicuous style of *Blood Meridian* generates a progressive as well as a conservative politics, so the self-conscious eclecticism of *Oscar Wao* is also open to positive besides negative interpretation, its meshing of innumerable voices from many cultural locations standing here for a democratic impulse, for liberation from what Linda Hutcheon calls 'the modernist ideology of artistic autonomy, individual expression, and the deliberate separation of art from mass culture and everyday life' (1989: 15).

To turn from McCarthy and Díaz to Silko, however, is to encounter a complete repudiation of flamboyant literary stylistics. If *Almanac of the Dead* is generous at the level of plot – its many story-strands extending across the Americas – it is miserly with regard to rhetorical and imagistic flourishes. The novel's opening paragraph can be taken as typical of its expressive mode:

> The old woman stands at the stove stirring the simmering brown liquid with great concentration. Occasionally Zeta smiles as she stares into the big blue enamel pot. She glances through the rising veil of steam at the young blond woman pouring pills from brown plastic prescription vials. (Silko 1992: 19)

The sheer functionality of the passage is striking, its 'colour' restricted to the browns, blues and blondes of the objects it describes. With this leaching-out of imagery, this reduction of language to its indicative or reportorial mood, Silko appears to be aspiring to what Roland Barthes famously calls 'writing degree zero' (1984: 72). The broad distinction that Barthes draws between 'writing' on the one hand and 'style' on the other is also suggestive for a reading of *Almanac of the Dead*. Whereas style is, according to this argument, something privatized, the individual author's 'glory' but also his or her 'prison' or 'solitude' (12), writing is defined by contrast as 'an act of historical solidarity' with others (15). Silko's renunciation of stylistic idiosyncrasy may be understood in this light as central to an attempt at reaching historically embattled Native American communities. It is unsurprising that she has referred elsewhere to how her own Pueblo people is especially concerned, in its linguistic practice, 'with story and communication', valuing most highly those words that are 'spoken from the heart, unpremeditated and unrehearsed' (Silko 1996: 49, 48). None of this is to say, however, that the model of language apparent in *Almanac of the Dead* itself is without difficulties. In the first instance, the novel can, as a substantial written performance, only gesture towards rather than directly replicate that situation of oral storytelling in which the verbalization most valued by the Pueblo people is likeliest to occur. Second, Silko's paring away of stylistic excess may have the effect of depriving her text of the politically progressive resources that, albeit provisionally, we have noted above in the conspicuous styles of both *Blood Meridian* and *Oscar Wao*.

Border-crossings

'We don't believe in boundaries. Borders,' says Calabazas, a Yaqui or Mexican Indian character living in Tucson, Arizona in *Almanac of the Dead*. 'Nothing like that' (Silko 1992: 216). Like the novel in which he figures, Calabazas imagines open, fluid geographies that exist beneath or across rigid political and military demarcations of space such as the border drawn between the United States and Mexico. All three of this chapter's novels, in fact, generate counter-cartographies of this kind, their spatial imaginations not bound by the coordinates of the US but, rather, tracking the varied passages of peoples, objects and ideas across the Americas (and sometimes beyond). All three novelists are, to borrow a phrase applied to McCarthy for *Blood Meridian*, writers of 'the *transfrontera* contact zone' (Eaton 2003: 174).

Among current critics, Paul Giles has been especially eloquent in pointing out the inadequacy of the nation-state as the intellectual basis of what is still called, dubiously, 'American Studies'. As he notes, a significant theoretical shift 'from nationality to estrangement' has brought into question 'conceptual categories bound up with custom and locality' (2001: 13). In this climate, 'disconcerting shadows' are cast over academic disciplines like American Studies that have, by tradition, been 'bound up with narrowly defined areas of indigenous principle' (13). Given their cross-border narrative concerns and their transnational stylistic resources, *Blood Meridian*, *Oscar Wao* and *Almanac of the Dead* are all well-equipped to satisfy a reconfigured model of the literature of the United States. It is noticeable, however, that constraints still apply upon the spatial freedom of these novels, with the transits across the Americas that they narrate continuing to be determined to a significant extent by the gravitational pull of the United States. In this negative respect, also, the novels may replicate the current state of American Studies. Astutely, Giles observes that the discipline's new interest in flows across borderlines has not always destabilized the category of the nation: 'impulses toward internationalism have consorted uneasily with powerful attachments to notions of local or national identity' (2001: 14). The US, in another critic's words, preserves both analytically and politically 'a residual force' (Siemerling 2005: 13). Equipped with a sense, then, of the difficult and multiple politics of border-crossing, we hope in this section to assess the variety and value of movements beyond the United States as they are traced in these three novels.

Emblematic of the geographical consciousness of this fiction is the fact, as noted above, that *Almanac of the Dead* begins not with narrative proper but with a map. Such a gesture is not necessarily, in and of itself, supportive of political critique. Geographers have long been sensitive to the ideological conservatism of maps, to the ways in which they serve the interests of oppressive forces. As J. B. Hartley writes, they tend to be products of social elites rather than 'popular, alternative, or subversive modes of expression. Maps are pre-eminently a language of power, not of protest' (1988: 301). Yet Silko's map in *Almanac of the Dead* is intended to go against the grain of this tradition of regressive cartography. Although it appears at first to be respecting the hegemony of the United States by placing Tucson very close to the centre of the double-page spread, its regional orientation means that the US as a whole occupies no more space than other countries. In large, upper-case lettering, the name of 'MEXICO' extends horizontally along the middle of the map. Additionally, inset portions of text identify other places relevant to the novel: the 'East Coast' of the US, to be sure, but also Haiti, Cuba, Colombia and Argentina. This sketching of alternative geographies then finds verbal support in the titling of the text's six parts: while the first is indeed called 'The United States of America', it gives way to parts with names such as 'Mexico', 'Africa' and 'The Americas'. If outward movement of this kind from a base in the United States potentially replicates an imperial trajectory, it is also readable, more progressively, as a thinning-out or muting of US power. For Ann Brigham, Silko's text is politically liberating in this way, resting on 'a model, not of expansion, but of expansiveness' (2004: 317).

The dissident quality of the map in *Almanac of the Dead* is apparent not only in its spatial layout but in its inscription of movement and change. Contesting the fixity of much cartographic representation, Silko's 'five hundred year map' is, as its heading suggests, oriented towards time as well as space. Virginia E. Bell describes it as 'a map of circuits', one which is attentive to 'paths of migration and travel' (2000: 18). Multiple dotted lines signifying those movements in which the novel will be interested criss-cross the US and Mexico border here (and often head further afield). The most progressive of these many transits is that of pan-Indian mobilization against the United States, summarized on the map as 'The Twin Brothers walk north with hundreds of thousands of people' (Silko 1992: 15). This particular direction of travel is in striking contrast to trajectories frequently encountered in US fiction (and in the nation's broader culture). While the power of the United States has often flowed south and west – orientations confirmed, for example, by the choice of 'west' as the last word of *Blood Meridian*'s own first chapter (14) – *Almanac of the Dead*, first in its map and then in its colossal narrative, proposes an alternative northern itinerary heading upwards from Mexico and other parts of Latin America.

At this point, however, we should be wary of finding in Silko's novel an uncritical celebration of border-crossing. What might be termed transnational space is never singular or simple, but, as one recent commentary by geographers puts it, actually *'complex, multi-dimensional and multiply inhabited'* (Jackson, Crang and Dwyer 2004: 3). As a corrective to the more euphoric of its own narratives of the porous *frontera* between the United States and Mexico, *Almanac of the Dead* offers abundant evidence that increasingly fluid movement across these national lines may also extend the means of exploiting and disciplining populations. Guns and other items useful to the repressive state apparatus travel as easily in the novel from the US to Mexico – confirming the 'popular perception of a transnational police state along the border' (Davis 2000: 36) – as armies of liberation pass in the opposite direction. Symptomatically, the bullet-proof vest worn with devotion by the Mexican arms dealer Menardo is non-indigenous, an item normally 'sold only to the US military and US police forces' (Silko 1992: 319). In addition, Silko writes vividly about what Mike Davis calls the 'Dickensian underworld of day labor' (2000: 93) that is to be found in the contemporary border economy. Where other novels of *la frontera* like T. C. Boyle's *The Tortilla Curtain* (1995) turn to realism in order to document the harsh conditions faced by transient labourers, Silko produces intensified images of the exploitation of workers' bodies by a vampiric transnational capital. A key figure here is the Arizona entrepreneur Trigg, for whom the underclass of nearby, easily accessible Mexico offers a resource for exploitation by his bio-materials enterprise: 'Hoboes or wetbacks could be "harvested" at the plasma centers where a doctor had already examined the "candidate" to be sure he was healthy' (1992: 663). This gothic twist to the narrative dramatizes the proliferation of US power in an era of intensified border-crossing, rather than its diminishing or curtailment.

Both *Almanac of the Dead* and *Oscar Wao* trace various turns taken by US imperialism in recent decades. Where Silko shows the exporting of the country's judicial and military apparatuses to Mexico, Díaz describes the effects on the Dominican Republic of that commercially driven mode of conquest which is sometimes called 'Coca-Colonization': for example, the emergence on Santo Domingo's streets, alongside local eateries, of 'US fast-food restaurants (Dunkin' Donuts and Burger King)' (Díaz 2008: 273). By comparison, *Blood Meridian* offers a kind of prehistory of such systematic and elaborate exertions of US power. Its setting, for the most part, in 1849 places it at a time still of territorial flux for the United States, with Texas and a substantial portion of the present-day South-western states having been acquired from Mexico only the previous year by the Treaty of Guadalupe-Hidalgo. During the novel, the beheading by Mexicans of the suggestively named Captain White and then the gradual attrition of Glanton's mercenary army might seem to suggest a stalling, even a reversal, of the might of the United States. In the main, however, *Blood Meridian* is ominously prophetic, its narrative of relatively small-scale adventurism beyond the nation's borders foreshadowing the progress of later, fully coordinated imperialist campaigns. There is an anticipatory quality in descriptions of 'the Americans' as 'months out of their own country' (McCarthy 1989: 177), or carrying 'war of a madman's making onto a foreign land' (40). Glimpsed in prototypical form here are advanced US incursions into the Americas, beginning with the Spanish–American War of 1898 centred upon Cuba, Puerto Rico and the Philippines and extending to Reaganite ventures of the early 1980s (for one critic, 'El Salvador's recent past lingers [...] in the violence that fills McCarthy's novel' (Shaw 2008: 228)). With the collecting by Glanton's gang of body parts from their enemies (McCarthy 1989: 78, 270), and the gang's merciless raids against encampments of the Gileños and Tiguas (155–60, 173–4), *Blood Meridian* also contains traces of the iconography of the Vietnam War of the 1960s and early 1970s. While it is overstatement to claim, as Vince Brewton does, that '*Blood Meridian* comes close to being a novel whose true subject is Vietnam' (2004: 123), it is undeniable that this later imperial venture is present, as eerie flashforward, amidst the period details of the text.

Such border-crossings in McCarthy's novel are unilinear, figured as assertions against another nation of the brute militaristic power of the US. Even where *Blood Meridian* sketches exchanges of a more fluid or reversible kind between cultures, the outcome is not usually progressive. Strikingly, several practices construed from at least the time of James Fenimore Cooper's *The Last of the Mohicans* (1826) to be alien to the Anglo-Saxon United States are shown in McCarthy's text as spilling over racial and national lines. It is 'the Americans' here, rather than Chihuahuans of either Spanish or Indian descent, who eat an antelope raw instead of subjecting it to the cookery that marks a developed society (129). Above all, it is they, not their enemies, who resort now to scalping. In all of these episodes, however, the criss-crossing of cultural lines carries a negative value: what Giles calls the 'indigenous principle' assumed and asserted by the United States from the time of its founding is unsettled, to be sure, but hardly in an emancipatory direction.

Nevertheless, extending our previous discussion of *Blood Meridian*'s complex and unstable politics, we might ask whether the novel also gestures towards border-crossings of a more progressive kind. Here some evidence is provided by the story-arc of the protagonist, named only as the kid, who begins with 'a taste for mindless violence' (3) but undergoes significant moral and political reconstruction. Marginalized, even absented, during the most graphic scenes of racialized violence enacted by Glanton's gang, the kid is, by the end, capable of regard for an old Mexican woman whom he finds seemingly still alive among a group of butchered pilgrims. There is pathos in the futility of his cross-cultural sympathy, the woman proving to be 'just a dried shell [...] dead in that place for years' (315). For one critic, the kid's trajectory from soldiering on behalf of Captain *White* (italics added) to such empathy towards a vulnerable Mexican woman amounts to an 'uncanny embodiment of a more diverse, proto-multicultural population on the frontier' (Eaton 2003: 163). This is, perhaps, over-optimistic, affixing McCarthy's novel too securely to a wholesome vision of ethnic and national interfusions. However, the argument does have the value of restoring to readings of *Blood Meridian* awareness of particular border-crossings that are in opposition to those imperialist lines of travel shown by the novel as radiating from the United States.

We wish to dwell for a moment on a particular aspect of the kid's confrontation with this woman from another country. Significantly, he addresses her not in English but in Spanish: 'Abuelita, he said. No puedes escúcharme?' (315). This switching of languages is entirely characteristic of *Blood Meridian*: from as early as Chapter II, when the narrative arrives in the borderlands between the United States and Mexico, McCarthy regularly incorporates sequences of untranslated Spanish. Restricted at times to single sentences of only half a dozen words, these passages are elsewhere quite extensive. Here is a report of the conversation of some Chihuahuan soldiers:

> Their talk when they talked was of witches or worse and always they sought to parcel from the darkness some voice or cry from among the cries that was no right beast. La gente dice que el coyote es un brujo. Muchas veces el brujo es un coyote.
> Y los indios también. Muchas veces llaman como los coyotes.
> Y qué es eso?
> Nada.
> Un tecolote. Nada mas.
> Quizás. (72)

While the Anglophone reader gratefully takes hold not only of 'coyote' but also of a word such as 'Nada' that is now part of familiar 'Spanglish' currency in the US/Mexico borderlands (and beyond), the effect of this and similar passages is still discomfiting. Like the soldiers sifting through the cacophony of night-time noises, readers without facility in Spanish have to try to find something of semantic significance amidst 'the darkness'.

McCarthy inaugurates here a bilingualism that he develops in subsequent work, notably in the novels, beginning with *All the Pretty Horses* (1992), which comprise the Border Trilogy. More to the point of the present discussion, he also anticipates in *Blood Meridian* Díaz's own experiments in the use of Spanish, first in the short story collection *Drown* (1996) and then, much more elaborately, in *Oscar Wao* itself. Like *Blood Meridian*, *Oscar Wao* frequently includes whole passages of untranslated Spanish. However, replicating his movement between high and popular cultures in the same portion of text, Díaz is also liable, more experimentally still, to alternate between English and Spanish within a single sentence. As evidence of how often his utterance becomes Spanglish in the novel, the following examples all come from the same two pages in which Lola, Oscar's sister, recalls her teenaged battles with their mother:

She wasn't una pendeja. I'd seen her slap grown men, push white police officers onto their asses, curse a whole group of bochincheras. (Díaz 2008: 59)

Figurín de mierda, she called me. You think you're someone but you ain't nada. (60)

When she threw away my Smiths and Sisters of Mercy posters – Aquí yo no quiero maricones – I bought replacements. (60)

Here and throughout the novel, Díaz renders textual space itself a border or hybrid zone, marked by the intersecting tracks of plural linguistic communities. Frequently comedic in register, the bilingualism of *Oscar Wao* carries nevertheless a radical political charge, serving to challenge English's normative power in the discourse of the United States. The untranslated words, appearing transgressively in Anglophone surrounds, stand perhaps for the ever-increasing 'foreign bodies' of Latino/a immigrants, whose arrival amounts to a 'reconquista' (110) reversing the direction of US ventures in the Americas. Díaz has, in fact, spoken in interview about the anti-colonial activism he intends through this disruption of English by Spanish: 'by forcing Spanish back onto English, forcing it to deal with the language it tried to exterminate in me, I've tried to represent a mirror-image of that violence on the page. Call it my revenge on English' (Céspedes and Torres-Saillant 2000: 904).

While *Almanac of the Dead* remains oddly Anglophone, both *Blood Meridian* and *Oscar Wao* take issue with a monoglot model of US literary composition. McCarthy's and Díaz's fiction can thus be aligned with a recent wave of scholarship dedicated to uncovering a sense of the multilingualism of the literature of the United States. Here we have in mind, for example, the pioneering editorial work of Werner Sollors and his colleagues at Harvard University, which has resulted in both *The Multilingual Anthology of American Literature* (2000) and a ground-clearing critical volume, *Multilingual America* (1998). Congruently, John Carlos Rowe has argued that scholars of US writing and other cultural forms 'need to see the study of languages not simply as the acquisition of useful tools, but as an integral part of their disciplines' (2002: xvii). Yet while both *Blood Meridian* and *Oscar Wao* echo this academic work in dethroning English from its absolute rule over the national literature, we should be careful to avoid too uncritical a celebration of their pluralizing of languages. For it is the case in each novel, especially McCarthy's, that English remains the linguistic norm, in relation to which Spanish is positioned as a variation. Fredric Jameson makes a similar point about the residual power of English in general during the current era of globalization that has otherwise seen an increased dissemination and hybridization of various tongues: in the same way that 'the United States is not just one country, or one culture, among others', so, Jameson writes, it is not yet the case 'that English is just one language among others' (1998: 58). We would argue, then, that the effects of the use of Spanish in this chapter's novels are still ambiguous rather than straightforwardly progressive. This is in keeping with the texts' ideological instability more generally, as we hope to demonstrate in a final section on their disparate versions of the history of the Americas.

The angel of history

Sterling, a Laguna Pueblo character in *Almanac of the Dead* overly given to thinking about figures from US history, such as the Native American leader Geronimo and the 1930s outlaw John Dillinger, turns to magazine articles in search of a cure. For improved 'mental hygiene', they advise him, 'one must let bygones be bygones' (36). There is no possibility, however, of either the character or the novel in which he appears relinquishing the historical habit. All three of this chapter's texts, in fact, have no hygienic defences to fight off infection by the history not only of the United States but of the Americas more broadly. *Almanac of the Dead* itself offers a genealogy of indigenous peoples that is explicitly positioned as counter to earlier, imperial histories. *Oscar Wao* is also dual in its temporal schema, combining a narrative of recent times in New Jersey with an account, going further and further back, of the past of the Dominican Republic. *Blood Meridian* presents itself still more directly as an historical novel, locating its action in three precisely specified moments – 1849, 1861 and 1878 – and drawing on an extensive archival record for its story of the marauding of Glanton's gang through northern Mexico. As John Sepich puts it in his painstakingly thorough examination of McCarthy's debts to documentary sources, an assessment of *Blood Meridian* 'as a work of pure fiction' is, while perfectly possible, 'an underinformed reading' (2008: 3). All three texts, then, are saturated by a sense of the past of the United States (and elsewhere), thereby aligning themselves with a turn in the nation's recent fiction that is also manifest in, for example, E. L. Doctorow's socialist counter-histories of the early twentieth century, Thomas Pynchon's and Don DeLillo's massive archaeologies of the US of the Cold War and after, and in revisionary historical novels by such African American writers as Morrison, David Bradley and Edward P. Jones.

These texts by McCarthy, Silko and Díaz share a concern not only with history itself, but with *historiography*: that is, the act or art of inscribing the past. A foregrounding of interest in the poetics and politics of historical reconstruction has been taken by Linda Hutcheon to be among the distinguishing marks of the postmodern novel. It is helpful to recall those historiographical questions which, according to Hutcheon, are brought to the surface by postmodern fiction that engages narratively with past times:

How can the present know the past it tells? We constantly narrate the past, but what are the conditions of the knowledge implied by that totalizing act of narration? Must a historical account acknowledge where it does not know for sure or is it allowed to guess? Do we know the past only through the present? Or is it a matter of only being able to understand the present through the past? (1989: 72)

Such questions are indispensable to discussion of this chapter's three novels. At first sight, however, only *Oscar Wao* among them would seem to fit securely within the category of playful and self-conscious novelistic writing about the past that Hutcheon calls 'historiographic metafiction' (14). Yunior, Díaz's main narrator, wonders several times, for example, where to begin the writing of Dominican history: 'There are other beginnings certainly, better ones, to be sure – if you ask me I would have started when the Spaniards "discovered" the New World – or when the US invaded Santo Domingo in 1916' (Díaz 2008: 211 n.23). This quotation is from one of many mock-academic footnotes running through the text that assemble a partial chronology of political events in the Dominican Republic against which are played out three genera-tions' personal dramas. In accord with Hutcheon's remarks on the self-questioning quality of postmodern historical fiction, *Oscar Wao* also acknowledges gaps, errors and uncertainties in its narra-tivization of the Dominican past. Yet none of this textual loosening is intended by Díaz to imply that history is therefore unattainable and unrepresentable. On the contrary, *Oscar Wao* is proof that acknowledging that the meaning of the past is 'unstable, contextual, relational, and provisional' (Hutcheon 1989: 67) makes its interpretation more rather than less pressing.

The kinds of playfulness and self-consciousness apparent in Díaz's novel are not replicated in the fiction by McCarthy and Silko. Nevertheless, *Blood Meridian* and *Almanac of the Dead*, too, are sensitive not only to the historical record but also to the circumstances and values of its narrativization in the present. For all the fidelity to documentary sources, McCarthy's novel still acknowledges its own constructedness: first by the elaborations of syntax and lexis discussed above, then by such features as the summaries of events – divided by dashes – which are placed at the beginning of each chapter. These bills of fare give off a suggestion of artifice, even pastiche; they have, in Judie Newman's words, a 'consciously archival' quality, which 'overtly aligns the novel with nineteenth-century forebears' (2007: 149). *Almanac of the Dead* is, notwithstanding its suspicion of a self-advertising stylistics, equally sensitive to its status as artful historical reconstruction. Allegorical of its own condition is the fact that the Native American almanac which is central to the plot is described as no longer an unimpeachably authoritative record of history, but, rather, as a document now fragmentary, fragile, heavily stained and covered with marginalia. Silko's text also discloses its work of historical revision when it interrupts narrative proper and includes, in chronicle form, an account of native resistances to white rule throughout the Americas from 1510 to 1945 (1992: 527–30).

The attention which postmodern historical fiction gives to the very processes and problems of writing history does not, Hutcheon argues, lead to hermetic textual play. Self-consciousness about the framing of historical reconstruction reveals – rather than deflects – ethical and political commitment; as Hutcheon says, improvising upon a famous remark by the Marxist theorist Fredric Jameson in *The Political Unconscious* (1981), 'History is not "what hurts" so much as "what we say once hurt" – for we are both irremediably distanced in time and yet determined to grant meaning to that real pain of others (and ourselves)' (82). This formulation is an apt one, specifically, for the novels by McCarthy, Silko and Díaz, since each is charged with a desire to represent the hurt of others in the past. *Blood Meridian* represents the historical borderlands of the US and

Mexico as, in effect, a war zone: 'the red land to the west' (281) or 'the bloodlands of the west' (138), replete with mutilated corpses and traumatized survivors. *Almanac of the Dead* situates itself explicitly as an act of memorialization, performing what Freud calls 'mourning-work' (Freud 2006: 312). For Freud, the subject in mourning finds the world 'become poor and empty' (313) after the loss of loved ones; and such is the state of the Americas in Silko's novel, depleted of its native inhabitants as the result of a brutal and rapacious white rule that has endured for five centuries. *Oscar Wao*, too, for all its fun with nerds and geeks, is haunted by historical victims. Symptomatically, 'Screams of the enslaved' (1), of those carried forcibly to the Americas from Africa, are cited in the novel's very first sentence.

The sensitivity towards history's casualties shown by all of this fiction brings to mind some words by the mid-century German Marxist theoretician, Walter Benjamin. Writing in 1940, with the ruins of World War II accumulating around him, Benjamin describes a painting by Paul Klee that shows an angel apparently transfixed by an object he is contemplating. The passage is worth quoting at length:

> This is how one pictures the angel of history. His face is turned toward the past. Where we perceive a chain of events, he sees one single catastrophe which keeps piling wreckage upon wreckage and hurls it in front of his feet. The angel would like to stay, awaken the dead, and make whole what has been smashed. But a storm is blowing from Paradise; it has got caught in his wings with such violence that the angel can no longer close them. This storm irresistibly propels him into the future to which his back is turned, while the pile of debris before him grows skyward. This storm is what we call progress. (1968: 257–8)

'Wreckage upon wreckage': the phrase is well-suited to the evidences of catastrophe assembled by this chapter's novels. The texts memorialize not only countless human casualties, but also, for example, vast buffalo herds in Texas reduced by an aggressive capitalism to 'crazed and sunchalked bones' (McCarthy 1989: 317), or mesas in New Mexico degraded to 'shattered, scarred sandstone' by mining for uranium used in the atomic bombs dropped on Japan (Silko 1992: 759). In the breadth and depth of its mourning, this fiction indeed has a face 'turned toward the past'. Yet Benjamin speaks also of the angel of history's irresistible propulsion towards the future. It remains, then, to consider the different forms of futurity that are glimpsed in these three historical novels; to ask whether the visions that are given of times to come may 'make whole what has been smashed'.

Of this chapter's texts, *Almanac of the Dead* is the one most driven by redemptive purpose. Earlier we saw that, at the level of the individual sentence, the novel is usually in the indicative or flatly descriptive mode; at the level of plot itself, however, the mood is often 'optative' or wish-fulfilling. A colossal effort of counter-factual storytelling is required, since 'Sixty million dead souls howl for justice in the Americas!' (Silko 1992: 723), the number put on suffering here echoing the 'Sixty Million and more' that, in Chapter 4, we saw cited by Toni Morrison at the start of her own revisionist history in *Beloved*. Justice, in *Almanac of the Dead*, will be delivered by Native American armies led from Mexico by the brothers Tacho and El Feo, assisted by groups of the militant dispossessed in the US, such as that gathered around the black Vietnam veteran Clinton (a constructive variation on the familiar traumatized type illustrated by *The Human Stain*'s Lester Farley). Ultimately, the revolution is not narrated: instead, this hectic and mobile novel ends in a gesture of tranquil circling-back, with the return of Sterling to the Laguna Pueblo lands in New Mexico from which he had been exiled. Yet *Almanac of the Dead* remains charged with optimistic and prophetic, or even messianic, force: elaborate as it is as an act of commemoration, its temporality is also crucially oriented towards 'the days yet to come' (137).

While the novel is indeed 'a radical rewriting of the past and future of the Americas' (Huhndorf 2009: 171), its narrative of the region is not without problems. At times, for example, it slides from critique of a socioeconomic system historically adminis-tered by whites towards a biologically based repudiation of 'the white man'. Its vision of cosmopolitanism, hybridity and migration rubs abrasively in places against residual impulses towards the nationalistic, the pure and the rooted. The text is therefore not immune to that paradoxical situation noted by Michelle Jarman, whereby the borderland between Mexico and the US has sometimes functioned not as a space for the refashioning of all fixed ethnic and cultural identities, but, rather, as 'an exclusionary site, where one's ethnicity and ideological stance against assimilation become dues of membership' (2006: 148). But while the stories told about race in *Almanac of the Dead* repay further discussion, we want to focus here on another narrative element that has occasionally attracted criticism: namely, the wish-fulfilling machinery itself that brings the elaborate systems of Euro-American capital to the brink of defeat by a motley guerrilla army. For the *New Republic*'s reviewer, cited by Shane Graham, this turn in the narrative 'is, frankly, naïve to the point of silliness. The appeal to prophecy cannot make up for the common-sense deficit' (2005: 76). Without dismissing entirely such an impatient reading, we prefer to approach this fantastical aspect of *Almanac of the Dead* via Jameson's nuanced reflections on narrative in the postmodern era. For Jameson, the rise of counter-factual storytelling can certainly be taken as evidence of a situation unpromising for direct political action: 'Fabulation – or if you prefer, mythomania and outright tall tales – is no doubt the symptom of social and historical impotence, of the blocking of possibilities that leaves little option but the imaginary' (1991: 369). Seen in this light, the fabulous tale of a multicultural revolutionary army in *Almanac of the Dead* lays bare the present lack of any plausible challenge to capitalism's rule in the Americas. Importantly, however, Jameson does not freeze discussion in the negative moment, but goes on to say that in counter-factual storytelling 'new multiple or alternate strings of events rattle the bars of the national tradition and the history manuals whose very constraints and necessities their parodic force indicts' (369). From this perspective, the prophetic narrative of *Almanac of the Dead* takes on a diagnostic quality, its very exaggeration serving to draw attention to the profound need for change, for challenge to the prevailing 'constraints and necessities'.

As in Silko's novel, storytelling in *Oscar Wao* takes an optimistic turn, offering what the text calls a 'counterspell' (Diaz 2008: 7). For the most part, the narrative is bleak, as it recounts a series of abuses by power in both the US and the Dominican Republic that ends with the murder of the loveable Oscar himself (322). And yet this deathly trajectory does not go unchallenged. Particularly important by way of corrective is the letter from Oscar that reaches Yunior in New Jersey some eight months after his death, reporting that he finally slept with Ybón, his great love in the DR. There are several reasons for caution: first, the letter's contestable status, given earlier, apparently contradictory, material in Yunior's own narrative (290);

second, the fact that a further package intended to say more never arrives from the Dominican Republic, leaving Oscar's account, like the almanac in Silko's novel, patchy rather than fully authoritative. Nevertheless, in a narrative saturated by death, the giving of the last word to a voice speaking euphorically from beyond the grave, as it were, cannot but be emancipatory. Oscar's letter is also no mere private matter, but potentially of political significance too. It ends with 'The beauty! The beauty!' (335), which looks like an exuberant and liberationist anti-colonial rewriting of 'The horror! the horror!' from Joseph Conrad's *Heart of Darkness* (1899), a novel often phobic in its construction of the world of the colonized.

By comparison with the counter-factual propensity of *Oscar Wao* and *Almanac of the Dead*, *Blood Meridian* is implacable in its sense of ominous historical tendencies. The novel opens on a morbid primal scene, showing the economic power of the United States as always a product of exploitative transnational processes: 'Blacks in the fields, lank and stooped, their fingers spiderlike among the bolls of cotton' (McCarthy 1989: 4). It ends pessimistically, too, describing a landscape full of 'violent children' (322) orphaned by the Civil War of 1861–5. In McCarthy's detail of a twelve-year-old boy 'inanely armed' (323) are the lineaments of the future military–industrial complex of the US that will not be accompanied by a moral sensibility of commensurate scale. The kid – that central character arguably prototypical of multicultural America – is murdered by the judge. There may, however, be political resistance in the novel's sheer piling-up of violences and victimizations, making it a poor vehicle for the celebration of US expansion that is often the ideological payload of the western. Judie Newman sketches an optimistic reading, too, of the half-page 'Epilogue', which departs from narrative proper and, in elliptical prose, describes 'wanderers' finding bones on 'the plain' (337). This ossuary of a landscape no longer seems a breeding-ground for a people destined to exercise imperial power. Newman links the passage to 'counter-narratives of Manifest Destiny in nineteenth-century literature', and argues that, 'Far from emphasizing the moment at which the United States apparently realizes the continentalist dream, McCarthy [...] shrinks empire down to the empty space of an animal boneyard' (Newman 2007: 149). Yet it is inappropriate to rest easily in this interpretation. The episode is, after all, a slight one, even its placement at the end lacking the power to undo that narrative of nascent US imperialism elaborated in the preceding pages. Also, the landscape of the West that Newman reads as telling of the decay of empire will, soon enough, house the atomic weaponry testing described so ominously in McCarthy's later novel, *The Crossing* (1994). Less 'an animal boneyard', then, than a dynamo for future expansions of the United States, many of them not merely regional in scope but, anticipating the concerns of our next chapter, global.

CHAPTER SIX

'IT'S THE END OF THE WORLD AS WE KNOW IT (AND I FEEL FINE)'?

GLOBALIZATION AND ITS DISCONTENTS IN *JASMINE* (1989) AND *COSMOPOLIS* (2003)

'It's a small world after all'

As contexts go they don't come much bigger than globalization. While 'postmodernism' was the academic buzzword of the 1980s it was overtaken by 'globalization' in the 1990s. Peter Dicken calculates that there were only thirteen publications with 'globalization' in the title '[b]etween 1980 and 1984 [...] Between 1984 and 1989 this rose to 78, but then from 1992 to 96 this rose to around 600 with 200 in 1996 alone' (2003: 7). In the introduction to *Globalization: The Key Concepts*, Thomas Eriksen complains that his office desk is 'groaning audibly' under the burden of a 'good-sized library on globalization, sorted roughly into about a dozen wavering stacks' (2007: ix). Eriksen works at the University of Oslo in Norway, but informs us that his desk was designed by Swedish engineers and the piles of books that are severely testing the office furniture are products of a transnational publishing industry. As a global phenomenon, we should note that globalization studies is part of the process it seeks to analyze. This branch of knowledge mirrors the key characteristics of its subject: size (as mentioned above, this is a big subject about a big subject); speed (this area of study has developed very quickly); mobility (the field is characterized by movement across international boundaries); and hybridity (diverse disciplinary combinations of cultural studies, economics, film, geography, history, literature, politics and sociology).

Arjun Appadurai, a leading authority on globalization, suggests that it:

has now become something of a truism that we are functioning in a world fundamentally characterized by objects in motion. These objects include ideas and ideologies, people and goods, images and messages, technologies and techniques. This is a world of flows. (2001: 5)

As an expert in the field, Appadurai (who was born in India, educated in Mumbai and Massachusetts and employed at universities in Chicago and New York) is invited to conferences around the globe to lecture to other academics on topics such as increasing global mobility. Demographic flows between countries and continents are taking place at unprecedented levels and involve a wide variety of people – academic globetrotters and mail-order brides, refugees and political exiles, seasonal farmers and short-break tourists. In 1950, the number of international tourist arrivals across the globe was around 25 million; by 2008, this figure had risen to 922 million (World Tourism Organization 2010). According to a census by the United Nations in 2005, there 'are now almost 200 million international migrants [...] more than double the figure recorded in 1980' (GCIM 2005). While tourism is a matter of leisure, international migration is mainly a matter of painful necessity as people struggle to escape war and persecution, famine and natural disasters, or seek better employment prospects. The transnational movement of workers is tied to a massive increase in the global flow of commodities. The volume of international trade increased almost twentyfold between 1950 and 2000 (Dicken 2003: 35). Multinational corporations were at the heart of this increase and are collectively responsible for around two-thirds of the world export of goods and services (52). The production of commodities and provision of services is increasingly transnational and networked. The manufacturing process may move a product across several national borders, so that, for example, a T-shirt made from Canadian cotton might be knitted in the Netherlands, dyed in Denmark, sewn in Sri Lanka, customized with a logo in Lagos and then shipped to a distribution centre in Delhi. The service industry is similarly 'deterritorialized' (not rooted to a single site), so that, for example, a call centre in India can offer information on insurance to customers calling at the same time from Indiana or Indonesia.

Insurance is one of a host of financial instruments that have increased massively in scale and mobility in recent times.

Globalization is often mentioned alongside the key terms 'financialization' and 'neoliberalism'. Financialization refers to the prodigious growth of financial products, markets and institutions. Over the last thirty years, banks and financial organizations have become increasingly conspicuous in the 'Global 500' list of the largest corporations. At the time of writing, there are four commercial banks in the top twenty and another fifty financial organizations in the complete list (Fortune 500: 2010). The growth of global banking has been promoted by the widespread adoption of neoliberal economic policies and in particular the deregulation of markets. Nation-states have aimed to minimize their intervention in the money markets and the financial sector has flourished accordingly: '[t]he total daily turnover of financial transactions in international markets, which stood at $2.3 billion in 1983, had risen to $130 billion by 2001' (Harvey 2005: 161). Each national economy is now deeply integrated in a transnational network of finance. The interconnectivity of circuits of capital is underlined by the current global economic crisis, which started in 2006 with US homeowners defaulting on sub-prime mortgages, rapidly escalated to the fall of major financial houses in North America, Europe and Asia and a subsequent worldwide recession.

Media reports on the economic crisis constitute one stream in another of the global flows identified by Appadurai: 'images and messages'. During the course of their everyday lives, many people in the developed world are assailed by information and audiovisual stimuli from computers and laptops, televisions and videogame consoles, mobile phones and PDAs, SatNavs and radios. Arguably, technology is *the* vital component in the processes of globalization. In particular, transport and telecommunications technology provide the pathways that facilitate the mercurial flows of people, commodities, capital, images and information across, beneath and above the surface of the globe. Cumulatively, these technologies result in a radical reconfiguration of space and time. An e-mail or text message sent to someone next door or on the other side of the world would arrive almost instantaneously. Critics have described these processes in terms of 'time-space compression' (Harvey 1989), the 'shrinking of the globe', the 'death of distance' (Cairncross 1997) and even 'the end of geography' (O'Brien 1992). Whichever terminology is used, most people seem to agree that the world is not as big as it used to be. Concurrently, there has been a significant increase in consciousness of global issues. Globalization is not only a series of material developments, but also a matter of changing perceptions and the burgeoning of a 'global imaginary': an enhanced awareness of interconnections and interdependence between people and places across the planet.

'Global terror.' 'Global warming.' 'Global economic crisis.' It is impossible to avoid the discourses of globalization and equally one can despair at the prospect of disentangling the rhetoric from the reality. The consensus view is that fundamental changes are taking place, but there is little agreement on the precise nature of these developments. The meaning of the keyword 'globalization' is itself fiercely contested. Some critics dismiss the term as a crude generalization, a 'fad word' (Bauman 1998: 1) or a 'myth' (Bourdieu 2003: 34). It has been contended that globalization is merely old wine in new bottles – fashionable jargon that obscures a long history of international migrations and trade. According to Immanuel Wallerstein, proponents of 'world-systems analysis [...] have been talking about globalization since long before the word was invented [...] not, however, as something new but as something that has been basic to the modern world system since it began in the sixteenth century' (2004: x). Colonialist and imperialist expansion from Europe into Asia, Africa and the Americas after 1492 generated deep networks of global interdependence. Marx might be regarded as a forerunner of world-systems analysis since, throughout his writing, he insisted that the '[t]he tendency to create the *world market* is directly given in the concept of capital itself' (1973: 408).

While some critics focus on the long history of capitalism and colonialism, others insist that contemporary globalization constitutes a decisive break with the past. Connections have always existed between far-flung places, but, it is argued, present-day global flows are unprecedented in their scale and scope. In the second half of the twentieth century, following decolonization and the fall of the Berlin Wall in 1989, postcolonial and former communist countries were systematically integrated into a single world market of historically unparalleled proportions and intra-connectivity. Responses to these developments are as sharply divided as opinions on the genealogy of globalization. The critical literature is vast and variegated but tends to point in one of two directions: globalization is either depicted as a homogenizing and essentially destructive force, or it is represented as a diversifying and primarily creative process. According to the former perspective, globalization typically involves the decimation of cultural and geographical difference. The colourings of local identity and regional particularity are erased by a blandly monochrome placelessness. Transnational corporations and telecommunications, tourism and consumerism combine to mass-produce what Marc Augé dubbed 'non-places': a geography of identikit supermarkets and malls, suburbs and airports, cinemas and fast-food restaurants (1995). Some of the most strident critiques of globalization come from the left and view this term as synonymous with capitalism and cultural imperialism, or 'Coca-Colonization' (an example of which we saw in the presence of Dunkin' Donuts and Burger King franchises on the streets of Santo Domingo in *Oscar Wao*) and 'McDonaldization' (a term coined by George Ritzer). The terminology here underlines the extent to which globalization for some is merely a repackaging of a specifically American capitalism and imperialism.

The anti-globalization position has been vigorously contested from various quarters, including some critics on the left. Hardt and Negri, alongside Appadurai and others, argue that traditional models of power that rely on a 'centre-margin' structure are redundant in a world now characterized by complex networks that are diffuse and decentred. In conjunction with this line of thinking, a number of studies in the field have focused on the potentially empowering and creative consequences of globalization. While not altogether denying the powerful shaping influence of transnational corporations and multinational media, this school of thought insists that homogenization is often counterbalanced, at ground level, by a heterogenization and hybridization of spaces and identities. According to this account, the proliferation of non-places is offset by the emergence of new 'glocal' geographies (a portmanteau term which refers to the customization of *glo*bal forces at the lo*cal* level) and Coca-Colonization is counterbalanced by the consumer's creative 'creolization'. In this alternative perspective on globalization, the vision of universally bland brandscapes and passive consumers is replaced by the possibility of localized resistance and recombinacy. The emphasis here is less on the destruction of authentic local cultures by global capitalism and more on how developments in transport and telecommunications have dramatically increased mobility and creative synergies between previously distant cultures.

Critics who subscribe to this view of globalization might point to the international success of hybrid cultural forms such as Bollywood cinema and 'world music'. Although the case studies in this chapter will focus on the literary representation of globalization, it is important to recognize that the novel as a material object is inextricably interwoven with these processes: relations of production, distribution and consumption in the literary marketplace are increasingly globalized. The *Harry Potter* books, for example, have been translated into over sixty languages and sold close to half a billion copies around the world. At a different point on the literary spectrum, we could also note a dramatic increase in global sales of, and prizes for, novels by writers from South America, Africa and Asia. One of the writers we will examine in this chapter, Bharati Mukherjee, has been the recipient of numerous prestigious awards for her fiction. Mukherjee prefers to be known as an American author although she was born in India, partly educated in England and lived in Canada for over a decade before migrating to the US. For some critics, the category of a singular and stable national identity is increasingly jeopardized by the forces of globalization. In this context the Palestinian American scholar, Edward Said, has proposed that globalization requires a fundamental revision of 'the idea that literature exists in a national framework' (2001: 64).

The question posed in 1863 by Julian Hawthorne has perhaps never been more urgently relevant than in the current era of globalization: '[w]hat is an American book?' (Hawthorne 2007: 43). A 'New' American Studies over the past twenty years has responded to this question by focusing on the 'boundaries between the local and the global, the national and the transnational' (Giles 2002: 286). In an important contribution to this field, *Fictions of Globalization*, James Annesley has argued persuasively that globalization has been a core concern in the fiction of American novelists over the past twenty years. We have already seen evidence of this in the critical engagement with transnational consumerism and brand culture in *Fight Club* and *American Psycho* as well as the mapping of geocultural interfaces in *Blood Meridian*, *Almanac of the Dead* and *The Brief Wondrous Life of Oscar Wao*. The focus of this chapter will be on two further contributions to the fiction of globalization: *Jasmine* (1989) by Bharati Mukherjee and *Cosmopolis* (2003) by Don DeLillo. *Jasmine* follows the journey of a young woman from a small rural village in India to a new life in the US, while

Cosmopolis centres on a day (the last day as it turns out) in the life of a multi-billionaire as his stretch limousine crawls across a gridlocked Manhattan. Mukherjee and DeLillo seem to offer radically different perspectives on globalization: one from below that traces trans-national migration and cultural exchanges at ground level and the other from above that belongs to the rarefied realm of finance capital and advanced technology. On the surface it might seem that these two texts are miles apart, one a story of the 'global village' and the other of 'global pillage' (to borrow Anthony Giddens's wordplay (2003: 11)); however, the processes of globalization forge connections between things, people and places which appear to be far apart and this will also be our aim in the following readings.

Jasmine, or How (not) to be a Postcolonial Pin-Up Girl for the Global Village

Bharati Mukherjee's life exemplifies the enhanced geographical mobility which characterizes the era of globalization. Born in 1940, Mukherjee has moved back and forth between India, England, Canada and the United States. Migration and cross-cultural exchange are core thematics in her writing and are central to *Jasmine*. The eponymous heroine is born in 1960 in the Punjab village of Hasnapur. Unlike the other women in this traditional rural community, Jyoti yearns for adventure. She marries Prakash, a 'modern man', and they move to the city of Jullundhar (Mukherjee 1991: 76). Prakash gives Jyoti a new name – Jasmine – and plans to escape with her from an India that is '"backward, mediocre, corrupt"' to a '"real life"' in America (81). However, Prakash is killed in a bomb attack by Sikh separatists and Jasmine, a seventeen-year-old widow, travels to the New World on her own. In Florida, she is given refuge by a Quaker woman who helps her to elude the immigration authorities, teaches her how to 'pass' as an American and gives her a new nickname, 'Jazzy'. Jasmine's next move takes her to New York where she works first as a domestic and then as an au pair for a middle-class family in Manhattan. Taylor Hayes, the father of the family, is attracted to 'Jase' (his pet name for Jasmine) and the two become close. Their relationship begins to blossom until a day out together in Central Park where Jasmine is shocked to see her husband's killer and runs away. Finding herself in Baden, a small Iowan farming community, Jasmine moves in with Bud Ripplemeyer and settles into a new life as 'Plain Jane' (another sobriquet). At the end of the novel, a recently divorced Taylor arrives with his son and Jasmine decides to leave with them. After multiple name changes and several thousand miles of travel, Jasmine is last seen heading west for the Californian coast.

Jasmine has proven very popular on university curricula, but critical opinion on the novel is sharply divided. A number of postcolonial critics have reproached Mukherjee for what they see as her uncritical endorsement of American mythology and colonialist ideology. Mukherjee became a US citizen in 1988 and for some critics *Jasmine* reads like a literary supplement to a green card in its enthusiastic embrace of its author's new homeland. To begin with, Jasmine's migration is mapped onto American romantic myths of mobility. The trajectory is not only from North to South but also from East to West across the Atlantic and the American continent. This direction is heavily freighted with mythic connotations as it mirrors the path taken first by the Pilgrim Fathers and then by explorers and pioneers during the era of westward expansion. Jasmine is traced through the stencil of American archetypes: a 'fighter and adapter', a Punjab pioneer who boldly sets off to explore unknown frontiers and create a new life for herself in the New World (40). In the course of her journey Jasmine is repeatedly recognized as unique and destined for better things: 'she is the brightest, the most educated, the bravest, the most "modern" of the village women. She is an American before the fact' (Koshy 1998: 147). As well as parroting the discourses of American exceptionalism, Mukherjee might be accused of sanctioning American individualism since the success story of a lone heroine who is 'greedy with wants' (Mukherjee 1991: 241) eclipses the collective sufferings endured by many migrants. Like a Hindu heroine dropped into a Horatio Alger tale, Jasmine goes from rags to riches – her journey is not only geographical but also racial and socioeconomic as she determinedly battles her way into the white American middle class. For Susan Koshy, *Jasmine* succumbs to the 'seductive appeal of the American Dream': the novel 'simultaneously attest[s] to the oppressiveness of India and the liberatory potential of America' (1998: 140, 147). America is positioned at the heart of the global village as the destination for those who want to break free from stifling traditions. Annesley echoes this claim by observing that *Jasmine* 'makes an equation between Americanization and globalization' (2006:

144). For Mukherjee, America is not just bound up with the fate of Jasmine but appears to be the manifest destiny of the world.

Alongside the valorization of American mythology, some critics have objected to the way Mukherjee's writing reinforces colonial ideology. Inderpal Grewal has dismissed *Jasmine* as a 'touristic text' (1994: 63), Kristin Carter-Sanborn accuses Mukherjee of 'pop multiculturalism' (1994: 66) and Rebecca Sultana derides the depiction of Hindu women and Sikh terrorists in India as 'nothing but ethnic caricatures' (2004: 106). While inter-ethnic violence is rife in India, there is almost nothing in *Jasmine* on racial conflict within the US. Jasmine does not encounter America's other 'others' – Native Americans, African Americans, Latino/as – and her own presence elicits very little hostility. Grewal offers a scathing rebuke of the fact that 'all white men fall in love with [Jasmine], and she possesses an ability to obliterate racism with the taste of the curry she makes for them' (2005: 68). Despite the fact that Jasmine cooks a meal for Bud which combines '[pot] roast and gobi aloo' (Mukherjee 1991: 213), Gurleen Grewal claims that Mukherjee serves the reader 'a spiced-up version of the classic recipe of assimilation into the dominant culture' (1993: 182). Jasmine's desire to fit in with the dominant culture is especially evident in the most multicultural location she passes through: New York. The South Asian community into which she moves is described ironically as a 'fortress of Punjabness' (Mukherjee 1991: 148): '[t]hey had Indian food stores in the block, Punjabi newspapers and Hindi film magazines at the corner stand, and a [Hindi] film every night' (145–6). Jasmine finds this 'artificially maintained Indianness' distasteful and decides to 'distance [her]self from everything Indian' (145). Against the claim that transnational migration produces cultural exchange and hybridity, *Jasmine* highlights the erasure of ethnic and racial differences in the process of migrant conformity.

Several critical readings of *Jasmine* have objected to its portrayal of America as the space of modernity in which 'immigrants are able to change their identities, whereas in India identities remain[ed] frozen' (Grewal 2005: 70). While migration is typically a matter of necessity, Mukherjee is reproached for representing it primarily as a 'process of self-invention and transformation' (1991: 34). As she moves west, Mukherjee's heroine metamorphosizes and assumes progressively more anglicized names – 'Jyoti', 'Jasmine', 'Jazzy', 'Jaze', 'Jane' – while wondering 'how many more shapes are in me, how many more selves, how many more husbands?' (1991: 215). The mutability of Jasmine's identity might be read as development from a passive and constrained Third World female subjectivity to that of an active First World feminist agent who shapes her own destiny. As well as regretting the implication that the First World has a monopoly on feminism, we might also note that the model of selfhood in *Jasmine* valorizes precisely those characteristics – mobility and adaptability – required of subjects in the global marketplace. Do the nimble geographical and cultural movements of the postcolonial nomad become a paradigm for a deterritorialized neoliberal subjectivity?

For some readers and critics, Mukherjee's response to globalization raises a series of politically problematic questions since it ventriloquizes dominant discourses and reproduces antipodes from the colonial imagination. Susan Koshy, for example, highlights the 'contrastive juxtaposition of an Indian past against an American present, Old World against New World', and insists that writers need to 'imagine in more complex ways the heterogeneous spaces of modernity' (1998: 150). In the reading of *Jasmine* that follows we do not intend to repudiate all of the criticisms sketched above, but we would like to suggest that, on closer inspection, parts of Mukherjee's novel contribute to a global imaginary which is more complex and less dualistic than Koshy allows. At one point in her relationship with Bud, Jasmine confesses that she envies 'the straight lines and smooth planes of his history' (Mukherjee 1991: 214). The image of globalization in *Jasmine* veers away from the geometry of tidy oppositions, 'straight lines and smooth planes', and towards a geography that is more tangled and rhizomatic. In key respects, Mukherjee's geographical imagination recalls the global imaginary offered by another Indian American, Arjun Appadurai. In place of a cartography of fixed points, Appadurai's mapping traces disorderly flows across a series of overlapping '-scapes': 'ethnoscapes', 'technoscapes', 'financescapes', 'mediascapes' and 'ideoscapes' (Appadurai 1990). The *ethnoscape* signifies 'the landscape of persons who constitute the shifting world in which we live: tourists, immigrants, refugees, exiles, guest-workers, and other moving groups and persons' (297). The *technoscape* refers to the global flows of technology, while the *financescape* is Appadurai's term for the indefatigable flows of capital across the globe. While the financescape is largely hidden (we will shortly see an attempt by DeLillo to drag it into the light), the *mediascape* is spectacularly visible. The global and increasingly integrated infrastructure of media and communications technologies facilitates the ceaseless flow of images in newspapers and magazines, on television and cinema screens, mobile phones and the internet. Appadurai's final category, the *ideoscape*, is closely related to the mediascape as a 'landscape of images' (299), but one that is more 'directly political [...] the ideologies of states and the counter-ideologies of movements' (300).

The signposts on the ideoscapes of *Jasmine* point in different directions. In places America is depicted in line with the dominant ideology as a borderless space of opportunity for risk-takers, but elsewhere we might describe Mukherjee's cartography as counter-hegemonic. When, for example, Jasmine first arrives in the US she is greeted by a blighted landscape and the echoes of earlier explorers setting foot in the New World are discordant:

> The first thing I saw were the two cones of a nuclear plant, and smoke spreading from them in complicated but seemingly purposeful patterns, edges lit by the rising sun, like a gray, intricate map of an unexplored island continent [...] I waded through Eden's waste: plastic bottles, floating oranges, boards, sodden boxes, white and green plastic sacks tied shut but picked open by birds and pulled apart by crabs. (95–6)

Following this ominous disembarkation, Jasmine's behaviour and experiences often suggest a critical distance from American myths of individualism and mobility. Rather than subscribing unconditionally to an individualist ethic, Mukherjee offers a heroine who is ethically ambiguous. Towards the close, Jasmine is about to set off on the road for a new life in California with Taylor: '[a]dventure, risk, transformation: the frontier is pushing through uncaulked windows' (240). At the same time, however, Jasmine is also running away from Bud – her paraplegic partner whose unborn child she is carrying. '[G]reedy with wants', Jasmine alludes to her destructive egotism: only '[t]ime will tell if I am a tornado, rubble-maker, arising from nowhere and disappearing into a cloud' (241). Before their departure Taylor advises his runaway bride-to-be that there is no need to pack: 'This is the age of plastic' (238). Although their destination is the West coast, Taylor's remark might return the reader to

Jasmine's arrival on the East coast's wasteland of 'white and green plastic sacks' and thus underline America's status as a throwaway culture where 'nothing lasts [...] the monuments are plastic [...] Nothing is forever, nothing is so terrible, or so wonderful that it won't disintegrate' (181). In America, disposability and impermanence are key features of landscape, relationships and individual identity. Mukherjee does not idealize her heroine's serial self-reinvention unequivocally: '[t]here are no harmless, compassionate ways to remake oneself. We murder who we were so we can rebirth our selves in the images of dreams' (29). The violence of identity is not exclusively existential, and in fact the multiple selves devised by the heroine might be seen as psychic defences against the physical trauma she experiences: we should not forget that Jasmine flees to America following the bomb blast that kills her husband, and that on her arrival in the US she is raped in a motel room and murders her attacker.

Mukherjee partly remaps, then, myths of mobility and selfhood on the American ideoscape with images of westering as wayward and violent. A similarly critical eye is cast over global ethnoscapes. Malini Johar Schueller notes that Mukherjee has been reproached for 'sugarcoating the immigrant experience' (2009: 92), but *Jasmine* does not cast migration naively as a romantic adventure of self-discovery. When she leaves India behind Jasmine discovers that perilous migrations are taking place on a massive scale:

> we are refugees and mercenaries and guest workers; you see us sleeping in airport lounges [...] We are the outcasts and deportees, strange pilgrims visiting outlandish shrines, landing at the end of tarmacs, ferried in old army trucks where we are roughly handled and taken to roped-off corners of waiting rooms, where surly, barely wakened customs guards await their bribe [...] We ask only one thing: to be allowed to land; to pass through; to continue. We sneak a look at the big departure board, the one the tourists use [...] What country? What continent? We pass through wars, through plagues [...] Whole peoples on the move. (101–2)

Passing through the 'shadow world' of 'phantom airlines' and 'nigger shipping', Jasmine meets '[h]ollow-eyed Muslim men in fur caps', a 'Filipina nurse', a 'Tamil auto mechanic', a Ugandan in a 'Mickey Mouse T-Shirt' who is wounded by the *Polizei* in suburban

Blankenese and a 'Surinamese Indian' working as a railway porter in Amsterdam (100–2). While some migrants, like Bud's adopted Vietnamese son, Du, have been displaced by war, others are looking for work. Jasmine's brothers plan to 'find jobs in a Gulf emirate' (46) while in New York she encounters a diasporic cohort of nannies working for white families that includes 'Letitia from Trinidad, and Jamaica from Barbados' (178). In New York she also meets another Asian migrant who works as 'an importer and sorter of human hair':

> Junk hair he sold to wigmakers. Fine hair to instrument makers. Eventually, scientific instruments and the US Defense Department. It was no exaggeration to say that the security of the free world, in some small way, depended on the hair of Indian village women [...] A hair from some peasant's head in Hasnapur could travel across oceans and save an American meteorologist's reputation. Nothing was rooted anymore. Everything was in motion. (151–2)

Global flows across transnational networks of production generate butterfly effects between people, objects and places across vast distances. Because nothing is rooted (not even, it seems, human hair), traditionally stable geographical markers such as 'here' and 'there' are jeopardized. Throughout *Jasmine* there are numerous examples of the interpenetration of Asia and America. Before she reaches US soil, Jasmine has already read an American novel (*Shane*) and seen a Hollywood film (*Seven Brides for Seven Brothers*). However, the mediascape is miscegenated since a motel in Florida has 'pink spiralling stairs [that] could have been straight out of an Amitav Bachchan film set' (111). The simple juxtaposition of East and West, North and South is undone by its refraction through a prism of transnational flows. New York is an 'archipelago of ghettos seething with aliens' (140) and even in the Midwest 'Bud Ripplemeyer has adopted a Vietnamese and shacked up with a Punjabi girl. There's a Vietnamese network. There are Hmong, with a church of their own, turning out quilts for Lutheran relief' which will be sent to famine victims in Ethiopia (229).

Before Jasmine can perform the archetypal American gesture of heading out west she has to get into Taylor's Toyota – a car designed, though not necessarily manufactured, in the East. The orientalist opposition of East and West is further unravelled by Mukherjee's mapping of the technoscape. Some Americans in the novel assume that India is a backwater: the rapist, Half-Face, is convinced that Jasmine has never seen a television set before arriving in the US. Conversely, Mukherjee traces a gallery of Asian characters who are attuned to electronic gadgetry. Jasmine's brothers are 'fixers and tinkerers [...] able to repair our storefront clinic's television set' (46), while her husband, Prakash, has 'a special talent for fixing televisions, VCRs, computers' (67). When the young couple go for scooter rides at the weekend they encounter a pervasive though unevenly distributed technological modernity: 'Shacks sprouted like toadstools around high-rise office buildings. Camels loped past satellite dishes' (80). Disjunctions are also evident in rural Iowa where the local farmers toil with heavy agricultural machinery while Du expertly retrofits domestic gadgetry: 'It's not engineering. It's recombinant electronics. I have altered the gene pool of the common American appliance' (156). Du, the Vietnamese war orphan, leaves home to study electrical repair at night school. Conversely, Darrel, an American farmer, is left stuck in Baden with his dream of moving to New Mexico to manage a Radio Shack. Unable to detach himself emotionally from his father's farm, local community and tradition, Darrel becomes depressed and eventually commits suicide. In terms of socioeconomic allegory, the moral here seems to be that an enervated and nostalgic white America might be left behind by a youthful, forward-looking and technophile Asia.

The changing contours of the technoscape in *Jasmine* are integrated with global flows of capital. Jasmine's life is framed by the financescape from an early age: 'When I was a child, born in a mud hut without water or electricity, the Green Revolution had just struck Punjab' (12). According to Matt Burkhart, the Green Revolution in India was 'spearheaded by US foreign aid agencies in conjunction with American agribusiness corporations [...] History has proven this program to be a thinly veiled effort to create markets for US agricultural technologies' (2008: 11). The massive influx of foreign investment resulted in a dramatic shake-up of farm ownership, techniques and technologies. Punjab was at the forefront of this disruptive modernization as farms were bought up and new machinery, fertilizers, pesticides and genetically modified seeds introduced to the region. Jasmine's father's farm is acquired by a man nicknamed 'Vancouver Singh' who had gone to 'agricultural school in Canada [...] was testing out scientific ideas [...] a new kind of wheat' and who also invests in 'an American-style "super-bazaar"' in Jullundhar (71). Vimla, one of Jasmine's friends in Jullundhar, is 'engaged to the son of the Tractor King of our district (he imported Zetta tractors from Czechoslovakia and was supposed to have illegal bank accounts all over Europe)' (75). The impact of flows of capital into and out of India during the Green Revolution stretched far wider than agricultural production. Burkhart makes a compelling link between investment in the region and increased unemployment among young men due to agglomeration economics – '[f]rom 1970 to 1980, the number of farms in Punjab dropped by 350,000' (2008: 14). Cumulatively these economic developments and the concomitant emergence of a commercial culture resulted in a resurgence of fundamentalism, inter-ethnic rivalry and crime (Vancouver Singh's farm is rumoured to be 'a safe house for drug pushers and gunmen' (Mukherjee 1991: 63)). The apparently 'local' clash between Sikhs and Hindus which claims Jasmine's husband is thus in fact contingent on the global expansion of capital.

Jasmine witnesses the social consequences of shifting finance-scapes in Iowa as well as India. Mukherjee establishes a deft spatial counterpoint between problems in Third World Punjab as it experiences investment inflow and First World Iowa undergoing investment outflow. When Jasmine arrives in Baden the traditional farming community is in conflict with the banks and the leisure industry: '[w]ith ground so cheap and farmers so desperate, [big developers are] snapping up huge packages for non-ag use [...] golf courses and water slides and softball parks' (10). As a local banker, Bud, Jasmine's husband, is a focal point for hostility in the farming community. One of his debtors shoots Bud in the back and another disgruntled farmer accuses him of conspiring with the 'Eastern banks': '[t]hey give the orders and he squeezes us, right?' (218). Jasmine's involvement in the financial sector predates her work as a bank teller in Baden. While in New York, she works as a language tutor for '[a] man with a Ford Foundation grant to study land reform in the Punjab [...] [and] executives being sent to Delhi' (180) as well as an economist who 'had been to India several times as a guest lecturer in Delhi, as a World Bank consultant, as a US government aid officer' and his wife who 'was a professor at NYU, but on leave to the World Bank, somewhere in West Africa' (181–4). Jasmine's journey is propelled by and intersects with powerful transnational energies, technologies and institutions. Mukherjee's heroine is too busy 'scrambling', as she describes it (241), to achieve an analytical distance from the financescapes, technoscapes, mediascapes, ethnoscapes and ideoscapes she crosses. *Jasmine* does not deliver a master narrative of globalization but instead aims to dramatize its centrifugal and centripetal forces as they conflict and converge: local and global, rural and urban, America and India, homogenization and heterogenization. These elements are not arranged as simple oppositions so much as intricately connected nodes on a network. On her first visit to an American mall, Jasmine is surprised first by a revolving door and then an escalator: '[h]ow could something be always open and at the same time always closed? [...] How could something be always moving and always still?' (133). Jasmine and *Jasmine* are drawn to an emerging global geography of simultaneity that deconstructs traditional antipodes.

Around the world in eighty nanoseconds: *Cosmopolis* and the space-time of globalization

Cosmopolis starts off where *Jasmine* ends – a journey westwards on the road – but while Mukherjee's story travels several thousand miles across continents, DeLillo's road novel stalls on Manhattan Island. The narrative charts one day in the life of 28-year old Eric Packer, a currency trader who has 'made and lost sums that could colonize a planet' (DeLillo 2003: 129). Packer lives in an East Side penthouse apartment that has forty-eight rooms including a shark tank, a screening room and two private elevators. On this 'Day in April [...] in the year 2000', he leaves his apartment to head across town for a haircut in a run-down barbershop in Hell's Kitchen (1). Packer's limousine crawls along 47th Street taking most of the day to cover around five miles. The trip is repeatedly interrupted: Manhattan is gridlocked by a Presidential cavalcade, a funeral procession for a rap star and an anti-globalization demonstration; Packer holds meetings with advisors, meets his doctor for a prostate check-up and has sex with several women; he attends a techno rave, is attacked by a pie-wielding 'pastry assassin', performs as an extra for a crowd scene in a film and murders his chief security officer. Although at the local level, the 'car move[s] at an inchworm creep' (64), state-of-the-art technology inside the limousine enables instant access around the globe: Packer watches news coverage of assassinations in North Korea and Russia, holds videoconferences and charts the global flows of currency. Throughout the day, he is speculating on the value of the yen and manages in the course of his visit to the barber to lose his entire fortune (to 'take a haircut' is slang for losing out on a financial deal). By the close of the day, Packer has shed almost all of his possessions and is shot in a derelict tenement by Richard Sheets (a.k.a. Benno Levin), an obsessive former employee. The thematic ground covered in *Cosmopolis* is well-trodden territory for DeLillo: byzantine connections between global capitalism, advanced technology and terrorist violence are central to several of his novels such as *The Names* (1982), *Mao II* (1991) and *Underworld* (1997). In the reading that follows we will make use once again of Appadurai's model of global flows but in reverse order from that in our consideration of *Jasmine*: starting with the representation of finance-, techno- and mediascapes before moving on to consider DeLillo's depiction of ethno- and ideoscapes.

Appadurai contends that 'global capital is now a more mysterious, rapid and difficult landscape to follow than ever before, as currency markets, national stock exchanges and commodity speculations move megamonies through national turnstiles at blinding speed' (1996: 34–5). The financescape is not only characterized by the unprecedented volume and velocity of capital, but also by exceptional levels of transnational integration. Operating with minimal regulatory interference by nation states, finance capital has consolidated and expanded to a level where it now dwarfs the 'real economy'. Dicken estimates that the ratio between financial speculation and trade in goods and services was around 2:1 in 1973 but had risen to 70:1 by 1995 (2003: 438). The prodigious reproduction of finance capital is largely incestuous and unrelated to material production. In other words, '[m]uch of the business of finance turns out to be about finance and nothing else' (Harvey 2005: 157). The market has witnessed an explosive proliferation of 'derivatives' which Scott Lash defines as 'bets on the sum of other people's bets' (2007: 18). Lash's terminology here tallies with Susan Strange's critique of 'casino capitalism':

> Every day games are played in this casino that involve sums of money so large that they cannot be imagined. At night the games go on at the other side of the world [...] [the players] are just like the gamblers in casinos watching the clicking spin of a silver ball

on a roulette wheel and putting their chips on red or black, odd numbers or even ones. (Strange 1997: 1)

'[B]etting against the yen', Eric Packer is a major player in this global casino (DeLillo 2003: 29). The insomniac Packer is able to gamble without pause since the '[c]urrency markets never close. And the Nikkei runs all day and night now. All the major exchanges. Seven days a week' (29). While playing for astronomical stakes in this virtual casino Packer is peculiarly averse to the tangible form of money. He carries 'no bills or coins' (129) on his person and looks disdainfully at the sight of money changing hands among street traders. This hostility extends to the language and technology associated with hard currency: Packer dismisses the acronym 'ATM' as 'aged [...] dated' (54) and suggests that cash registers ought to be 'confined to display cases in a museum' (71). The multi-billionaire financier seems to want to follow his 'cyber-capital' out of the 'age of industrial glut into the smart spaces built on beams of light' (102), a realm 'beyond geography and touchable money and the people who stack and count it' (36). Packer's winnings in this rarefied domain depend on his ability to predict the 'movements of money itself' as it becomes ever more mobile and immaterial (75). Following on from shells and coins to paper notes and plastic cards, finance capital appears to represent the future mutation of money into pure information. This future is written on the side of an office building on Broadway before which Packer stands transfixed:

> three tiers of data running concurrently and swiftly about a hundred feet above the street. Financial news, stock prices, currency markets. The action was unflagging. The hellbent sprint of numbers and symbols, the fractions, decimals, stylized dollar signs [...] The speed is the point [...] pure spectacle, or information made sacred, ritually unreadable. (80)

Packer's 'chief of theory', Vija Kinski, underscores the extent to which this info-capital is self-referential and largely disconnected from human discourse and agency: 'Money has lost its narrative quality [...] Money is talking to itself' (77).

Changes in the circuitry of capital on the global financescape are integrated with dramatic developments on the technoscape:

Travelling at the speed of light, as nothing but assemblages of zeroes and ones, global money dances through the world's fibre-optic networks in astonishing volumes [...] National boundaries mean little in this context: it is much easier to move $41 billion from London to New York than a truckload of grapes from California to Nevada. (Cited in Dicken 2003: 442)

In the mid-90s the top ten US and European banks spent around $22 billion on information technology (Dicken 2003: 442), and 'by 2000, IT accounted for around 45% of all investment' (Harvey 2005: 157). The computer systems of banks and other financial organizations form a labyrinthine digital network of ceaselessly circulating info-capital. In *Cosmopolis*, Packer informs his currency analyst, Michael Chin, that '[f]or someone your age, with your gifts, there's only one thing in the world worth pursuing professionally and intellectually [...] The interaction between technology and capital. The inseparability' (23). Packer himself is virtually inseparable from technology: from his cyborg-like dependence on multiple screens and telecommunications devices inside his apartment and mobile office to the electron camera inside a wristwatch that is 'so microscopically refined it was almost pure information [...] almost metaphysics' (204). One consequence of his intimacy with screens is that Packer's experience of places and people comes to be framed by, and as, a mediascape. While the anti-globalization protests are taking place, Packer turns from the events themselves to watch the live coverage on TV. During the funeral of Brutha Fez, Packer wants to 'see the hearse pass by again, the body tilted for viewing, a digital corpse, a loop, a replication. It did not seem right that the hearse has come and gone' (139). And later, when he takes part in a crowd scene for a film, Packer's vision is filtered through a cinematic *mise-en-scène*: 'there were many different shades of skin colour but he saw them in black-and-white and he didn't know why' (176).

Cosmopolis highlights the symbiosis between bodies, technology and consciousness and hints at imminent cyber-utopian possibilities. Rather than opposing the technoscape with nature, Packer sees the global flows of financial data as:

soulful and glowing, a dynamic aspect of the life process. This was the eloquence of alphabets and numeric systems, now fully realized in electronic form, in the zero-oneness of the world, the digital imperative that defined every breath of the planet's living billions. Here was the heave of the biosphere. Our bodies and oceans were here, knowable and whole. (24)

Kinski speculates that the next stage in this process will involve the death of computers – which in the age of global networks are already practically redundant as 'distinct units' – followed by the downloading of human consciousness into a cyberspace where 'never-ending life begins' as the soul is absorbed in 'streams of information' (104). While these cyberspace prophecies might appear chimerical, *Cosmopolis* makes it clear that technological advances have already produced a 'new fluid reality' (83) characterized by the radical compression of space and time. The TV and computer Packer has inside his wristwatch transports his gaze instantaneously across a globe that figuratively shrinks to the size of a miniature screen. Surrounded by telecommunications technologies that bring the world to him, Packer asks at one point: 'Why do we still have airports?' (22).

As well as shaping geography in its own image, technology also streamlines the temporal by dramatically accelerating the rhythms of everyday life. Packer is successful because he is synchronized with the new temporality of info-capital. While others in the market study patterns over 'years, months, weeks', he looks for 'hourly cycles. Then stinking minutes. Then down to seconds' (37). In discussion with Kinski, Packer even defines the duration of a 'nanosecond', 'zeptosecond' and 'yoctosecond' (respectively one billionth, one sextillionth and one septillionth of a second). In *Cosmopolis,* technology threatens to speed up time to the point at which the present might race ahead of the future. On two occasions, Packer experiences an uncanny flashforward. The first occurs during the anti-globalization demonstration when Packer watches himself on webcam as he recoils at an explosion a few moments *before* the blast. A second series of bizarre prolepses takes place in the closing scene as Packer witnesses his own death on the screen in his wristwatch: an ambulance, a morgue, an identification tag and then, cryptically, in the novel's final lines: 'He is dead inside the crystal of his watch but still alive in original space, waiting for the shot to sound' (209).

The closing sentence of *Cosmopolis* crystallizes a central opposition within the text. Packer is left poised precariously between two worlds, two temporalities. On the one hand, the wristwatch displays a postmodern space-time: inside the crystal of the future we glimpse a virtual sphere that belongs to cyber-capital and technology and which is smooth and weightless, digital and hyper-accelerated. Underneath the digital wristwatch, however, there is a second hand, one which is wounded (Packer shoots himself through the palm) and belongs to an 'original space'. DeLillo juxtaposes the postmodern and postindustrial chronotope with a modernist and industrial space-time: beneath the frictionless and hyper-mobile networks of finance capital there lies a big city, sticky and striated, territorially embedded, seething with bodies that move in time to an older urban-industrial clock. The curve of *Cosmopolis* takes Packer away from postmodern space-time and global finance and down to street level where he can begin the 'business of living' (107); the reader follows this trajectory away from New York as the global hub of cyber-capital and towards New York as a 'World City' (the literal meaning of 'Cosmo-polis').

Once he leaves his penthouse and limousine, Packer is caught up in 'the great rapacious flow [...] the physical will of the city' (41) and plunged into a crowded multicultural ethnoscape that 'eats and sleeps noise' (71). At each stage in his urban odyssey, he collides with ethnic and cultural diversity: as his chauffeur, Ibrahim Hamadou, drives past the United Nations secretariat, Packer can hear 'stray words in French and Somali' and see '[d]ark women in ivory robes [...] Irish nannies pushing strollers' (17). They drive past a 'tour bus with Swedes and Chinese' (34) and tourists swarm around the megastores in the Theatre District and the streets of Little Tokyo. In the course of the day Packer encounters a smorgasbord of food cultures: French, Greek and Ethiopian restaurants, a taco cart and a Mexican grocery. The culmination of this brush with the hetero-geneity of the World City is the funeral of Brutha Fez. The passing of an African American singer who performed 'Sufi music, rapping in Punjabi and Urdu and in the black swagger English of the street' (133) is honoured by a procession that dramatizes New York's status as a diasporic crossroads for demographic and cultural flows: 'foreign dignitaries, faces from film and TV, and mingled throughout were figures from world religion in their robes, cowls, kimonos, sandals and soutanes' (135).

Packer's reaction to 'the huddle of old cultures' in the World City (66) is both ethnically and sexually conflicted. Driving through the Diamond District he is revolted by the street traders like the Hasidim who haggle over

> a form of money so obsolete Eric didn't know how to think about it. It was hard, shiny, faceted. It was everything he'd left behind or never encountered, cut and polished, intensely three-dimensional. People wore it and flashed it. They took it off to go to bed or have sex and they put it on to have sex or die in. [...] Cash for gold and diamonds. Rings, coins, pearls, wholesale jewelry, antique jewelry. This was the souk, the shtetl. Here were the hagglers and talebearers, the scrapmongers, the dealers in stray talk. The street was an offence to the future. But he responded to it. He felt it enter every receptor and vault electrically to his brain. (64–5)

While the abstract numbers of transnational cyber-capital 'talk' to themselves, trade in the local marketplace continues to involve human discourse and bodily contact unmediated by technology. Inside the hygienic cocoon of his high-tech limousine, Packer observes 'medleys of data on every screen [...] The context was nearly touchless. He could talk most systems into operation or wave a hand at a screen and make it go blank' (13). Although Packer declares that 'Freud is finished' (6), one might offer a psycho-analytical gloss on the multi-billionaire's aversion to 'touchable money and the people who stack and count it' (36). An emotional investment in the sanitary sphere of virtual capitalism over the marketplace where money and goods change hands might suggest psychosexual repression. Freud drew on a long-established tradition in folklore and mythology of associating money with excrement as 'filthy lucre'. According to psychoanalysis, an equation can be drawn between the infantile response to faeces and the adult relation to money, especially among those who hoard or 'hold in' their wealth. Packer's desire to distance himself from the tactile form of money in favour of data on a screen might be symptomatic of a puritanical touch phobia. In this regard it is significant that Packer's assassin and double loves to play with the symbolic equivalent of shit: Richard *Sheets*, in an act of infantile regression, relishes the materiality of money by licking and biting coins and fantasizes about stealing money from Packer's dead body 'for its personal qualities [...] I wanted its intimacy and touch [...] I wanted to rub the bills over my face to remind me why I shot him' (58).

Although Sheets confesses that he was instructed to shoot Packer by a fungus on his toe, he also confronts the multi-billionaire with a more obviously political justification for his assassination, one which takes us unequivocally onto the novel's ideoscape: 'For the limousine that displaces the air that people need to breathe in Bangladesh. This alone' (202). Sheets aims to legitimize terrorist violence by reference to transnational connections between extremes of wealth, poverty and environmental damage. The pseudonym adopted by Packer's assassin, 'Benno Levin', alludes to the figurehead for the fundamentalist backlash against globalization (bin Laden) and the two other assassinations that take place on the same day in *Cosmopolis* involve the same political target. The first victim is Arthur Rapp, the managing director of the International Monetary Fund (IMF), and his shooting in Nike, North Korea, is witnessed live on the Money Channel by a global audience. The second victim is 'Nikolai Kaganovich, a man of swaggering wealth and shady reputation, owner of Russia's largest media conglomerate, with interests that ranged from sex magazines to satellite operations' (81). In the media coverage of the media tycoon's assassination, there is speculation about 'anti-globalist elements and local wars' (82). In a surreal dress rehearsal for his subsequent shooting, Packer is also attacked by André Petrescu, 'the pastry assassin' (142). Wearing, ironically, a 'Disney World T-shirt', Petrescu stalks a gallery of global celebrities that includes 'corporate directors, military commanders, soccer stars and politicians' and hits them in the face with pies: '[t]his is my mission worldwide. To sabotage power and wealth' (142).

Earlier in the day, at the anti-globalization demonstration, the tactics of the protestors ranged from the slapstick surrealism of Petrescu to the terrorist violence of Benno Levin. The key motif during this urban uprising is the rat: some of the participants wear spandex rat costumes and carry a giant Styrofoam rat, while others release rats in restaurants and onto the streets. A stock ticker above 47th Street is reprogrammed to display an enigmatic notice: 'A RAT BECAME THE UNIT OF CURRENCY' (96). This quotation from a poem by Zbigniew Herbert about the siege of a Polish city by the Nazis links finance capitalism to fascist dreams of global domination and replaces the image of money as pure data with the symbol of a scavenging rodent. On a second electronic display the protestors revise the opening sentence of *The Communist Manifesto*: 'A SPECTRE IS HAUNTING THE WORLD – THE SPECTRE

OF CAPITALISM' (96). Packer recognizes both allusions, and the fact that they identify him as the enemy is further underlined by the protestors' bombing of an investment bank, the storming of the NASDAQ stock exchange and an attack on his limousine. Like the historical event upon which it is loosely based – the Battle for Seattle in November 1999 – the demonstration in *Cosmopolis* brings together an eclectic mixture of Marxists, anarchists and environmentalists who are united in their opposition to capitalism as the economic engine of globalization.

Global media coverage of the protests around the World Trade Organization meeting in Seattle introduced many people to the anti-globalization movement. In *Cosmopolis*, DeLillo maps the political clash between globalization and its discontents onto frictions between the ideoscape and the mediascape. Kinski proposes to Packer that battle lines in the conflict over globalization are not clearly drawn and in fact the protestors can be dismissed as:

a fantasy generated by the market. They don't exist outside the market. There is nowhere they can go to be outside. There is no outside [...] They are necessary to the system they despise. They give it energy and definition. (90)

For Kinski the protest functions as an inoculation which invigorates the immune system of the global market and testifies 'for the ten-thousandth time, to [its] innovative brilliance, its ability to shape itself to its own flexible ends, absorbing everything around it' (99). Packer objects by focusing on the most disturbing event in the protest: a man's self-immolation: 'Now look. A man in flames [...] Kinski had been wrong. The market was not total. It could not claim this man or assimilate this act [...] This was a thing outside its reach' (99–100). In retaliation, Kinski informs her employer that this man is merely copying media images of Vietnamese monks performing anti-war protests in the 1960s. For Kinski there are no authentic or original subversive acts, only the replaying of media clichés and 'quotations from someone else's life' (85).

Cosmopolis intimates that there 'is no outside' from which to oppose the capitalist world system since a hyper-real mediascape has transformed everything into spectacle. At the same time, however, DeLillo hints that the system may already be against itself. The head of Packer Capital embodies the system of global finance and it is clear that he desires his own extinction. When he murders his chief of security it becomes evident that Packer wishes not only to lose his fortune but his life. A parallel might be drawn here between Packer and the narrator in *Fight Club* who similarly suffers from insomnia and attempts to bring down the system as it is embodied within him. Like Palahniuk's conflicted protagonist, Packer attempts to escape the hyper-real sphere of images and 'live in meat space' (DeLillo 2003: 64) – working his way back into the body through sex and sadomasochistic violence that includes self-inflicted stigmata (shooting himself in the hand). As Packer's road trip slides into a death drive, we might speculate that *Cosmopolis* is implicitly rewriting another quotation from Marx and insinuating that globalization contains the seeds of its own destruction. The novel's historical setting is significant in this respect. In interview, DeLillo identified 'April 2000 [as] the moment when the financial market collapsed, when recession took over from years of enormous growth. That was the end of a world' (cited in Crosthwaite 2008: 8). *Cosmopolis* takes place at the precise moment when stock markets, having reached record highs, were poised on the brink of a spectacular fall. Packer's reckless gambling leads to:

> currencies tumbling everywhere. Bank failures were spreading. He found the humidor and lit a cigar. Strategists could not explain the speed and depth of the fall [...] He was so leveraged, his firm's portfolio so large and sprawling, linked crucially to the affairs of so many key institutions, all reciprocally vulnerable, that the whole system was in danger. (115–16)

In his reading of *Cosmopolis*, Paul Crosthwaite describes this phenomenon as a 'global accident' – a term that originates from the work of Paul Virilio. In *Unknown Quantity* (2003), Virilio proposes that new technologies have produced the conditions in which accidents are no longer necessarily restricted to the local or regional scale. The profound interconnectivity of global systems makes them increasingly vulnerable to cascade effects as was illustrated by the bursting of the 'dotcom bubble' in 2000 and again during the financial meltdown that started in 2006. It is important, however, to draw a distinction here between structural instability and autoimmunity. Rather than evidence of the seeds of self-destruction, the global accident may in fact be a vital component in the functioning of the system. In *The Shock Doctrine* (2007), Naomi Klein offers a strident critique of an emergent 'disaster capitalism' for which the global accident is a structural necessity. Packer's instruction to his female bodyguard to shoot him with her one-hundred-thousand-volt stun gun might thus be read as a surrogate death wish, or merely a mode of (kinky) reinvigoration.

We started this section by noting that *Cosmopolis* picks up where *Jasmine* left off, on a westerly road trip. In some respects the trajectories traced by the protagonists point in opposite directions: the female migrant from the Third World is heading towards a new life while the multi-billionaire westerner is about to die. At the same time, the global imaginary in Mukherjee and DeLillo shares key features: both represent globalization as a complex series of intersecting flows between people, capital, technology, media images and ideology; both illustrate that globalization can involve homogenization and heterogenization, destruction and creativity, violence and opportunity; both demonstrate, crucially, that globalization is not a singular and unified phenomenon so much as an ensemble of processes that are unevenly distributed and far from complete. In addition, we should note a final significant point at which these apparently contrasting texts converge. Fiction and other cultural productions do not simply deliver a passively detached reflection on the processes of globalization, but rather they comprise a critical contribution to the ongoing construction of a global imaginary.

REVIEW, READING AND RESEARCH

Chapter 3: Overpowering Consumerism

Review

- Massive increases in consumption in post-war US society constitute a critical context for any consideration of contemporary fiction.
- Recent novels have gravitated towards the visual culture of consumer society – the almost irresistible power of media, advertising and brands.
- This chapter's novels share a sense that the real world of material objects has been replaced by a numbing phantasmagoria or 'hyper-reality' of images. Ellis and Palahniuk consider violence both a structural component of the consumer society and a potential means of escape.
- The erotic economy of consumer society is shown to revolve around 'pornification', the sexualization of commodities as fetishes, compulsive seriality and sadomasochistic desire.
- Political opposition to consumer society is problematized by the suspicion that there is no longer a recognizable 'outside' to the system – even the practice of critique appears to have been incorporated and commodified.

Reading

Annesley, J. (1998), *Blank Fictions: Consumerism, Culture and the Contemporary American Novel*. London: Pluto.

Baudrillard, J. (1998), *The Consumer Society: Myths and Structures*. Thousand Oaks, CA: Sage.

—(2003), The Violence of Images. http://www.egs.edu/faculty/jean-baudrillard/articles/the-violence-of-the-image/.

—(2005), *The System of Objects*. London: Verso.

Benjamin, W. (1999), *The Arcades Project*. Cambridge, MA: Belknap Press.

Ellis, B. E. (1997), *American Psycho*. London: Macmillan (first published 1991).

Fitzgerald, F. S. (1990), *The Great Gatsby*. London: Penguin (first published 1925).

Gaitskill, M. (1998), 'The Dentist', in *Because They Wanted To*. New York: Simon & Schuster (first published 1997).

Jameson, F. (1991), *Postmodernism, or, The Cultural Logic of Late Capitalism* London: Verso.

Klein, N. (2001), *No Logo*. London: Flamingo.

Mailer, N. (1992b), 'A note on comparative pornography', in *Advertisements for Myself*. Cambridge, MA: Harvard University Press.

Murphet, J. (2002), *Bret Easton Ellis's American Psycho: A Reader's Guide*. New York: Continuum.

Palahniuk, C. (1999a), *Fight Club: A Novel*. New York: Henry Holt & Company.

Young, E. and Caveney, G. (1994), *Shopping in Space: Essays on America's Blank Generation Fiction*. New York: Grove Press.

Research

- Look for examples in contemporary American fiction of things, places and people which stand *outside* consumer society. A good place to start this search would be Don DeLillo's *White Noise* (1985).
- Often obsessed with consumerism, contemporary American fiction pays very little attention to the largely invisible infrastructure of *production*. Why are there so few novels about the world of work? Can you locate any fictions of labour on the contemporary American scene?
- This chapter focused on two novels by male authors. Do men and women respond differently to consumerism? In this regard, was the contrastive example mentioned between Bushnell's *Sex and the City* and McCarthy's *The Road* instructive or misleading?

Chapter 4: Between Black and White

Review

- Race is not one topic among others in American fiction but is always present, whether explicitly or implicitly.
- Recent scholarship on race has rejected 'essentialist' understandings of racial differences denoting fixed essences, whether biological or cultural, arguing that race is a category we bring to the world rather than something we find in it.
- African American slavery is central, rather than peripheral to modernism and modernity.
- Whereas earlier liberal attempts to overcome racism tended to adopt a 'colour-blind' approach, emphasizing similarity rather than difference, identity politics and multiculturalism have aimed to overcome racism by foregrounding difference.
- With its attachment to distinct and defining identities, identity politics is in potential tension with a theoretical emphasis on the contingent and constructed character of race.

Reading

Gates, H. L., Jr. (1997), 'The passing of Anatole Broyard', in *Thirteen Ways of Looking at a Black Man*. New York: Random House, pp. 180–214.

Gilroy, P. (1993), *The Black Atlantic: Modernity and Double Consciousness*. London: Verso.

Hall, S. (1996), 'Cultural identity and cinematic representation', in *Black British Cultural Studies: A Reader*. Chicago: University of Chicago Press, pp. 210–22.

Kaplan, B. A. (2005), 'Anatole Broyard's Human Stain: performing postracial consciousness'. *Philip Roth Studies* 1, 2: 125–44.

King, M. L. (2000), *Why We Can't Wait*. New York: Penguin.

LaCapra, D. (1991), 'Introduction', in D. LaCapra (ed.), *The Bounds of Race: Perspectives on Hegemony and Resistance*. Ithaca: Cornell University Press.

Luckhurst, R. (2008), *The Trauma Question*. Abingdon: Routledge.

Morrison, T. (1987), *Beloved*. London: Vintage.

—(1989), 'Unspeakable things unspoken: the Afro-American presence in American literature'. *Michigan Quarterly Review* 28: 1–34.

—(1993), *Playing in the Dark: Whiteness and the Literary Imagination*. London: Picador.

Perez-Torres, R. (1999), 'Between presence and absence: *Beloved*, postmodernism, and blackness', in W. L. Andrews and N. Y. McKay (eds), *Toni Morrison's Beloved: A Casebook*. New York: Oxford University Press, pp. 179–201.

Roth, P. (2001), *The Human Stain*. London: Vintage (first published 2000).

Royal, D. P. (2006), 'Plotting the frames of subjectivity: identity, death, and narrative in Philip Roth's *The Human Stain*'. *Contemporary Literature* 47, 1: 114–140.

Research

- Look carefully at the narrative forms of *Beloved* and *The Human Stain*, their shifts in time and perspective. How do these shifts relate to the novels' key themes?

- Consider the representation of and relationship between history and identity in the other two novels of Roth's 'American Trilogy', *American Pastoral* (1997) and *I Married A Communist* (1998), and in Morrison's novels *Jazz* (1992) and *Paradise* (1999).

- Look carefully at descriptions in American literature of how racial differences are experienced. Do such descriptions portray racial categories as natural and inevitable or as socially constructed and imposed?

- Compare the depiction of passing in Roth's *The Human Stain* with that found in earlier African American-authored novels about passing, such as Nella Larsen's *Passing* (1929) or James Weldon

Johnson's *The Autobiography of an Ex-Colored Man* (1912). What differences can you find, and how might you account for these?

Chapter 5: The Contemporary Americas Novel

Review

- It is important to recognize conceptual and political problems in assuming that 'America' means 'United States'. We should aim to position US literature and culture more generally within the regional context of 'the Americas'.
- Recent American fiction has displayed a heightened interest in 'border zones', particularly those between the US and Mexico.
- The thematic and political concern with cultural and geographical 'crossings' is mirrored in the very form of border fictions as they cross between genres, discourses and languages.
- Border fictions may also be characterized by a degree of ideological disunity. As we saw in the case studies, the very procedures of border fiction may sometimes mimic imperial itineraries or continue to grant political and cultural sovereignty to the region's superpower.
- The contemporary Americas novel is typically driven by heightened historical and archaeological impulses. Border fictions catalogue an enduring history of white violence in the Americas and also gesture towards the possibility of vengeance and redemption.

Reading

Anzaldúa, G. (1987), *Borderlands / La Frontera: The New Mestiza*. San Francisco: Aunt Lute Books.

Brigham, A. (2004), 'Productions of geographic scale and capitalist-colonialist enterprise in Leslie Marmon Silko's *Almanac of the Dead*'. *Modern Fiction Studies* 50, 2: 303–31.

Celayo, A. and Shook, D. (2008), 'In darkness we meet: a conversation with Junot Díaz'. *World Literature Today* 82, 2: 13–17.

Díaz, J. (2008), *The Brief Wondrous Life of Oscar Wao*. London: Faber and Faber (first published 2007).

Eaton, M. A. (2003), 'Dis(re)membered bodies: Cormac McCarthy's Border Fiction'. *Modern Fiction Studies* 49, 1: 155–80.

Holloway, D. (2002), *The Late Modernism of Cormac McCarthy*. London: Greenwood Press.

Huhndorf, S. M. (2009), *Mapping the Americas: The Transnational Politics of Contemporary Native Culture*. Ithaca: Cornell University Press.

Jameson, F. (1998), 'Notes on globalization as a philosophical issue', in F. Jameson and M. Miyoshi (eds), *The Cultures of Globalization*. Durham, NC: Duke University Press, pp. 54–77.

Jarman, M. (2006), 'Exploring the world of the different in Leslie Marmon Silko's *Almanac of the Dead*'. *MELUS* 31, 3: 147–68.

McCarthy, C. (1989), *Blood Meridian, or, The Evening Redness in the West*. London: Picador (first published 1985).

Newman, J. (2007), *Fictions of America: Narratives of Global Empire*. Abingdon: Routledge.

Saldívar, J. D. (1997), *Border Matters: Remapping American Cultural Studies*. Berkeley: University of California Press.

Sepich, J. (2008), *Notes on Blood Meridian* (revised edn). Austin: University of Texas Press.

Silko, L. M. (1992), *Almanac of the Dead*. New York: Penguin (first published 1991)

Research

- Broaden your border-crossing horizons by considering other fictions from this burgeoning oeuvre, such as: Cormac McCarthy's Border Trilogy (*All the Pretty Horses* (1992), *The Crossing* (1994) and *Cities of the Plain* (1998)), William Vollmann's *Imperial* (2009) and Oscar Hijuelos's *Beautiful Maria of My Soul* (2010).

- Both *Blood Meridian* and *Oscar Wao* make significant use of passages of untranslated Spanish. Research other examples of contemporary American fiction in which languages besides English are used, and evaluate the cultural and ideological implications of these practices. A starting point might be T. C. Boyle's own use of Spanish in *The Tortilla Curtain*.

Chapter 6: 'It's the End of the World as We Know It (and I Feel Fine)'?

Review

- It is important to position US literature and culture more generally within the transnational context of globalization.
- In the age of globalization, people and capital, commodities and technology, images and ideologies move ever more speedily within and across the boundaries of nation-states.
- Globalization is also characterized by increasing interconnectivity across vast distances. In this regard we need to recognize

the critical importance of the space-shrinking technologies of travel and telecommunications.

- The critical literature on globalization can be broadly divided into two schools: the first insists on destructive and homogenizing forces while the second looks to the possibility of creative and diversifying energies.
- Globalization is best understood as a conflicted and continuous process rather than a completed state of affairs.
- Contemporary fiction plays an important role in the ongoing construction of a global imaginary.

Reading

Annesley, J. (2006), *Fictions of Globalization: Consumption, the Market and the Contemporary American Novel.* London: Continuum.

Appadurai, A. (1990), 'Disjuncture and difference in the global cultural economy'. *Theory, Culture & Society*, 7: 295–310.

—1996, *Modernity at Large: Cultural Dimensions of Globalization.* Minneapolis: University of Minnesota Press.

Burkhart, M. (2008), 'Rewriting the West(ern): Shane, Jane, and Agricultural Change in Bharati Mukherjee's Jasmine'. *Western American Literature*, 43,1: 5–22.

Connell, L. and Marsh, N. (eds) (2010), *Literature and Globalization: A Reader.* Abingdon: Routledge.

DeLillo, D. (2003), *Cosmopolis.* New York: Scribner.

Dicken, P. (2003), *Global Shift: Reshaping the Global Economic Map in the 21ˢᵗ Century.* London: Sage.

Grewal, I. (2005), *Transnational America. Feminisms, Diasporas, Neoliberalisms.* Durham, NC: Duke University Press.

Gupta, S. (2009), *Globalization and Literature.* Cambridge: Polity.

Hardt, M. and Negri, A. (2001), *Empire.* Cambridge, MA: Harvard University Press.

Harvey, D. (2005), *A Brief History of Neoliberalism.* Oxford: Oxford University Press.

Klein, N. (2007), *The Shock Doctrine: The Rise of Disaster Capitalism.* New York: Metropolitan Books.

Mukherjee, B. (1991), *Jasmine.* London: Virago (first published 1989).

Ritzer, G. (2005), *The McDonaldization of Society 5.* Los Angeles: Pine Forge.

Schueller, M. J. (2009), *Locating Race: Global Sites of Post-Colonial Citizenship.* New York: SUNY Press.

Wallerstein, I. (2004), *World-Systems Analysis: An Introduction.* Durham, NC: Duke University Press.

Research

- Is it still possible to talk about the 'American' novel in the age of globalization?
- Does the contemporary American novel depict the processes of globalization as primarily destructive and homogenizing or, alternately, as creative and diversifying?
- To consider this question, other fictions of globalization that you may wish to take into account include: DeLillo's *Underworld* (1997); Joseph O'Neill's *Netherland* (2008) (which bears interesting comparison to *Cosmopolis* in its depiction of post-9/11 New York as a World City); Thomas Pynchon's *Against the Day* (2006) (or, indeed, this author's pioneering contributions to the literary crafting of a global imaginary in *V* (1963), *Gravity's Rainbow* (1973) and *Mason & Dixon* (1997)); and William Gibson's *Pattern Recognition* (2003).
- Alternatively, in place of these canonical names, you might consider the deterritorializing of the contemporary American novel by less well-established immigrant authors such as Daniel Alarcón (*Lost City* (2007)), Olga Grushin (*The Dream Life of Sukhanov* (2007) and *The Line* (2010)), Aleksandar Hemon (*The Lazarus Project* (2008)), Téa Obreht (*The Tiger's Wife* (2011)), and Gary Shteyngart (*Absurdistan* (2008) and *Super Sad True Love Story* (2010)).

PART THREE

WIDER CONTEXTS

CHAPTER SEVEN

AFTERLIVES AND ADAPTATIONS

THE CONTEMPORARY AMERICAN NOVEL ON FILM, VIDEO AND THE INTERNET

Hollywood and the contemporary American novel

From its very beginnings, commercial cinema in the United States has turned to the adaptation of novels in an attempt to burnish its own products with literature's high cultural prestige. Given Hollywood's organizing of itself from early in the twentieth century as a colossal storytelling factory, it is unsurprising that it has also regarded literary fiction as so much exploitable narrative property. This economically driven interest in a pre-existing stock of stories is, if anything, now more intense than ever. For novels have not only narrative DNA which is compatible with the system of commercial US cinema, but also extensive readerships, significant fan communities, even devoted cults (*Fight Club*, perhaps, or *American Psycho*), whose members can confidently be expected to follow the transition of a text to other media platforms such as film.

Adaptation is often, Linda Hutcheon writes, 'a transgenerational phenomenon' (2006: 32). There is interest in seeing what happens to classic novels when they are adapted in later periods informed by very different models of class, gender and race. However, cinematic adaptation does not always operate across such significant gaps in time. Hollywood's eye for already-formed narratives means that novels may now be repurposed as films within a few years of their appearance, considerably reducing possibilities of transgenerational reinterpretation. The rapidity and scale of the process can be gauged by citing some US novels from the period covered by this book that have been adapted for the screen. The list that follows is arranged chronologically according to the novels' date of publication (the second date in each case being that of the film version):

- Marilynne Robinson, *Housekeeping* (1980; 1987)
- John Irving, *The Hotel New Hampshire* (1981; 1984)
- Alice Walker, *The Color Purple* (1982; 1985)
- Jay McInerney, *Bright Lights, Big City* (1984; 1988)
- Bret Easton Ellis, *Less Than Zero* (1985; 1987)
- Bobbie Ann Mason, *In Country* (1985; 1989)
- Tom Wolfe, *The Bonfire of the Vanities* (1987; 1990)
- Fannie Flagg, *Fried Green Tomatoes at the Whistle Stop Cafe* (1987; 1991)
- Bret Easton Ellis, *The Rules of Attraction* (1987; 2002)
- E. L. Doctorow, *Billy Bathgate* (1989; 1991)
- Jane Smiley, *A Thousand Acres* (1991; 1997)
- Cormac McCarthy, *All the Pretty Horses* (1992; 2000)
- Amy Tan, *The Joy Luck Club* (1993; 1997)
- Jeffrey Eugenides, *The Virgin Suicides* (1993; 1999)
- Annie Proulx, *The Shipping News* (1993; 2001)
- Charles Frazier, *Cold Mountain* (1997; 2003)
- Michael Cunningham, *The Hours* (1999; 2002)
- Cormac McCarthy, *No Country for Old Men* (2005; 2007)
- Cormac McCarthy, *The Road* (2006; 2009)

To this already lengthy catalogue should be added recent US fiction dubiously categorized as 'popular' or 'genre' that has also proved amenable to film adaptation (everything from crime novels like *L.A. Confidential* to globetrotting conspiracy thrillers like *The Bourne Ultimatum*). The list is open-ended, too, not including films scheduled for future release, such as David Cronenberg's version of *Cosmopolis* (due in 2011).

Given the impossibility of addressing so many adaptations, we focus here on some questions raised by the cinematic reworking of four novels discussed in this book's middle chapters. David Fincher's version of *Fight Club* in 1999 will be paired with Mary Harron's of *American Psycho* the following year; Jonathan Demme's 1998 adaptation of *Beloved* will, more briefly, be juxtaposed with Robert Benton's 2003 film of *The Human Stain*. At this point, however, it is important to stress the limitations of approaching each film simply through its relationship to a source-novel. On the contrary, these films are also cannibalizations of numerous other cultural materials: 'it serves us better', as Julie Sanders says, to think 'in terms of intertextual webs or signifying fields, rather than simplistic one-way lines of influence from source to adaptation' (2006: 24). Thus, for example, the viewer of Fincher's *Fight Club* might see the film as overlaying not merely the novel by Palahniuk but also the director's previous account of contemporary urban and gender crises in *Se7en* (1995).

Four film adaptations

In a sense, the screen adaptations of Ellis's *American Psycho* and Palahniuk's *Fight Club* only formalize the books' already-cinematic quality. When the narrator ('Joe') likens Tyler Durden's hitting him to 'a cartoon boxing glove on a spring on Saturday morning cartoons' (Palahniuk 1999a: 53), or Patrick Bateman frames a murderous spree as scenes from a supercharged action movie (Ellis 1997: 335–8), the novels unveil their incorporation of film as both stylistic resource and archive of allusions. One of Tyler's strategies of social subversion, in the Palahniuk novel, even takes specifically cinematic form. In his job as a projectionist, he cuts frames from pornography into family-oriented entertainment:

> Tyler spliced a penis into everything after that. Usually, close-ups, or a Grand Canyon vagina with an echo, four stories tall and twitching with blood pressure as Cinderella danced with her Prince Charming and people watched. (31)

Tyler's practice has an unsettling effect upon spectators, causing them to 'feel sick or start to cry' (31). The moment is a suggestive one in the present context, prompting us to ask whether the adaptations themselves of *Fight Club* and *American Psycho* activate their own strategies of destabilization. Without resorting quite to Tyler's obscene tactic, are these films able nevertheless to disrupt the complacency of contemporary image culture and carry across to the screen that social criticism which in Chapter 3 we found, albeit partially, in the source-novels?

For Fincher and Harron, both opportunities and dangers arise from what was described above as contemporary consumerism's prioritizing of the visual. Positively, it means their work can immediately engage the commodity world on its preferred ground, as against Palahniuk's and Ellis's still clunky verbalization of images. The risk, however, is that their films may end up reproducing consumerism's glossy visuals, rather than undoing them. As it happens, both of these adaptations are indeed criss-crossed in contradictory fashion by progressive and conservative impulses. Harron's film has a liberating effect through its refunctioning of regressive visual materials. The shots from a porn movie and *The Texas Chain Saw Massacre* that play in the background as Bateman, respectively, makes a phone call and works out are diminished here in both scale and consequence, their reactionary politics challenged now that they are self-consciously 'quoted'. Her medium's visual properties also allow Harron to be subversive in staging Bateman's sex scene with 'Christie' and 'Sabrina'. While still in danger of advancing that narcissistic body culture we discuss below, the shots of a naked Bateman gazing at his own reflection in mirrors rather than at the women dramatize nicely the claustrophobic, self-referring qualities of contemporary consumerism's visual regime.

The bold critique of the image apparent here can be found, too, at moments in the adaptation of *Fight Club*. Take what is perhaps its most famous scene: the montage in which the apartment of the narrator ('Jack', rather than the novel's 'Joe') is filled by a succession of furnishings from IKEA. Each of these items is less a practical thing than a costly spectacle luring the film viewer too and, potentially, repressing his or her critical faculties. Yet two elements in the staging of this sequence impede the spectator's capitulation to image culture: first, the accompanying of each object on screen by its considerable price tag, alerting us to the stubborn fact of uneven wealth distribution; second, the counterpointing of image by sound, since this lavish styling of Jack's home is undercut by his sardonic voiceover.

At times, however, the two films may carry the virus of consumerism, rather than its antidote. This seems an especially counter-intuitive proposition in the case of the adaptation of *American Psycho*. Given such compositional features as Christian Bale's stylized performance as Bateman and the merciless excerpting of his banal musical tastes on the soundtrack, the film would appear to operate uncomplicatedly as a skewering of the world of conspicuous consumption. The satirical intention is even, for some critics, too blatant: Nick James writes of Harron that 'You immediately feel her art-crowd contempt for the cityboy' (2000). Other aspects of the film, however, compromise its progressive quality. Here we could address its paradoxical place within the consumer economy it seems to assail: its identity as not only a profit-seeking object itself, but one orbited by product spin-offs (including the charming Bateman doll mentioned in Chapter 3). But more damaging still are ambivalences in the film's representational choices themselves. While some major brands including Calvin Klein refused permission for Harron to show(case) their products, others were less reticent: the credits offer fawning thanks to the likes of Cerruti (for the bespoke clothing worn by Bateman's circle). Indeed, the camera seems at least half in love with this commodity world, registering the contours, colours and textures of expensively designed suits and foodstuffs. If the adaptation refuses the novel's repellent details of misogynistic violence, it also, more troublingly, declines to find an equivalent for the novel's nauseous inventories of opulent consumer brands. The 'Morning' chapter of Ellis's *American Psycho* is stuffed with brand names over four, barely tolerable pages (1997: 24–7), as if giving the reader an excess of consumerism in a desperate attempt at cure; the 'Morning' sequence of Harron's has its satirical touches, to be sure, but is altogether much less purgative.

The adaptation of *Fight Club*, too, may contribute in some measure to the social malaise it seeks to diagnose. Even putting to one side the political incoherence of its narrative – something shared with the source-novel – we may still find the film less transgressive of consumerism than its enthusiasts believe (Amy Taubin claims that it 'expresses some pretty subversive, right-on-the-zeitgeist ideas about [...] our name-brand, bottom-line society' (1999)). Consider, for example, how its sustained use of low-key lighting may amount to a stylish repetition of the look of film noir, only drained now of noir's political force. The run-down urban environment in which Fight Club and Project Mayhem are hatched looks like a well-financed filmmakers' simulation of a slum, echoing the night-time alleyway – all subtle lighting and smoky atmospherics – in which Bateman carries out his first murder in *American Psycho* the movie. While it is readily apparent that the adaptation of *Fight Club* is edgier in cinematic idiom than *American Psycho*, it is less certain that the frenetic camerawork and staccato editing are endowed with radical ideological purpose. A conjunction of cinematographic liveliness and political quietude might be sensed in an early moment characteristic of Fincher's *mise-en-scène* when a shot zooms rapidly through and out of an office waste-basket filled with rubbish, including coffee cups, soft drinks cans and a Krispy Kreme Doughnuts bag. Certainly, the case can be made that the shot's unnerving speed and detail jolt the spectator into registering the detritus of consumer society; a more compelling argument, however, is that the shot communicates more vividly still its own stylishness, the sheer panache of the technical manoeuvre displacing analysis of this ill-functioning commodity world and, incidentally, serving to consolidate Fincher's own brand-identity as a director.

And then, in each film, there is the conspicuous presentation of finely chiselled male bodies. By showing minimally or not at all gross sexual violences against women, the adaptation of *American Psycho* jams, on the whole, voyeuristic impulses that may be activated in the reader of Ellis's novel. Although it is at the cost of weakening the scandalous links Ellis makes between compulsory consumerism and compulsive violence (something discussed in Chapter 3), the decision which Harron and her co-screenwriter Guinevere Turner make not to restage the novel's disassembly of women's bodies is clearly motivated by feminist reluctance to import into their work the slasher genre and its dubious sexual politics. 'As a result', writes David Eldridge, 'the only object in the film that could be described as pornographic is Bateman himself, fetishized in the display of Christian Bale's buff body' (2008: 24). Undressed male bodies are to the fore as well in the film of *Fight Club*, presented by the camera with a detail not matched by the relatively spare prose of Palahniuk's novel. While not all of these bodies have the requisite toning, the series culminates in the lean, sculpted figure of Brad Pitt himself as Tyler, naked from the waist up. Taubin is driven to evoke 'a wet-dream half light that gilds the men's bodies as they pound each other's heads into the cement' (1999). There is certainly ample room here for interpretations interested in uncovering subtexts of the homosocial, even the homoerotic. Yet what may be disclosed by the image of Pitt, and that of Bale in *American Psycho*, is less the reconfiguring of gender and class relations than, disappointingly, the ever-increasing reach of advanced consumerism. The (wet) dream now is of the commodified male body itself, the designer torso existing as the latest consumer product to be gazed upon and desired.

In adapting *American Psycho* and *Fight Club*, Harron and Fincher were working with novels that had a considerable media buzz and boasted near-cultic readerships. By contrast, Jonathan Demme and Robert Benton and their screenwriters faced the problem, in their versions respectively of *Beloved* and *The Human Stain*, of translating to the screen novels already of high canonical status by senior US writers. Unfortunately, there are lingering effects here of early cinema's attempt to ameliorate its own 'vulgar' status by turning too respectfully to literature for its material. Both films have a surfeit of deference and tastefulness. Although Mia Mask has tried to recruit Demme's *Beloved* to experimental cinema – calling it 'an avant-garde (read art-house) film' (2005: 276) and 'an aesthetically and ideologically progressive project' (286) – her argument is deeply unconvincing. The film is, on the contrary, thoroughly 'Hollywoodized' in its narrative patterning, stylistic repertoire and ideological implication. Only in such elements as the horror-movie presentation of Beloved herself, Thandie Newton's voice recalling that of the possessed girl in *The Exorcist* (1973), does the work break free of its middlebrow shackles and recall Demme's own beginnings in the energetic exploitation flick (such as the delirious genre hybrid *Crazy Mama* (1975)). More characteristic of the film is the moment when Sethe (Oprah Winfrey) reveals the scarring on her back, the soft, flattering lighting here like that recommended for a successful dinner party. This kind of lighting design can be found, too, in Benton's adaptation of *The Human Stain* (as during de-eroticized sex scenes between Anthony Hopkins as Coleman Silk and Nicole Kidman as Faunia Farley). The two films are united as well in having Rachel Portman as their composer: her delicate piano, strings and woodwind orchestrations are merely wistful, collaborating with other aspects of storytelling and *mise-en-scène* to purge the source-novels of their potentially militant, transgressive force.

For reasons of space, we confine ourselves here to comparison of the novels' and films' narrative modes. Even if currently in progress in Western culture is a general domestication or naturalization of jagged artistic forms – once-subversive fractures and discontinuities now looking routine in our dizzying world – *Beloved* the book is still unsettling in its non-linear composition. *Beloved* the movie, by contrast, is very orderly, any movements from the present into the past bridged by the voice of Sethe or Paul D. Helpful as this technique is to spectator understanding, it nevertheless has the effect of smoothing out the African American experience of slavery, rather than showing, as Morrison does, its ungovernable temporality, its disruptive cuts into post-Abolition life. The adaptation of *The Human Stain* uses flashback to similarly undemanding effect, and is also notable for how it swerves past vexed issues of focalization in Roth's original. Where the novel presents, as discussed in Chapter 4, a series of overlapping, sometimes contradictory perspectives, the film has no interest in pursuing the question of 'who sees?'. An example of this active simplification can be found in its staging of the memorial service for Silk. Benton shows the African American Herb Keble lamenting his earlier reluctance to support Silk; the moment is left at that, mending interpersonal relations. Things are, however, a good deal more complex and troubling in Roth's text: while reporting the same words from Keble that we encounter on screen, Nathan Zuckerman, as framing narrator, wonders about the lateness and futility of this reparative gesture, and concludes, 'Fuck him' (312).

Further evidence of these two films' consoling reorientations of narrative can be found by considering their endings. Demme's *Beloved* does not reproduce the open-endedness of Morrison's novel, the sense of unappeased African American trauma; instead, the film concludes with a long shot of Sethe's house in daylight, this image's optimistic effect augmented by birdsong on the soundtrack. Benton ends his version of *The Human Stain* with a shot of Coleman and Faunia dancing together on Zuckerman's porch. The two central characters are thereby unified after death, in a wish-fulfilling gesture which resolves any tensions of race, class and age. As with *Beloved* the film, the effect, finally, is of a glib, personalized solution to the structural dilemmas charted by the literary source. None of this discussion, of course, is intended to generalize about the relative powers of literature and cinema – but merely to sketch the dubiously therapeutic effects of these two film adaptations in particular.

Adaptation and participation

Productively, Linda Hutcheon distinguishes between three types of activity, or 'modes of engagement', generated by adaptations (2006: 27). First among these modes is 'telling', as with those adaptations that take the form of novels (or novelizations); second is 'showing', as when the prior text is reworked as a play or film. There is, however, a third sort of engagement solicited by adaptation, which Hutcheon calls 'participating' (12), or 'interacting with stories' (27). While the dividing lines between these categories are more broken than she allows – only an inert reader of a novel would not also 'participate' in some way while still being subjected to 'telling' – her typology is very helpful for our purpose here of sifting various reinterpretations of contemporary US fiction.

Already in this chapter, we have discussed adaptations in the mode of 'showing' (and to the lengthy list of films might be added other reworkings of novels for an audience, such as the Broadway musical of *The Color Purple* that ran in 2005). We also need, however, to comment briefly on adaptations of novels in the mode of 'participating'. Even while employing this useful category, it is important to distinguish between the very different texts and activities that may be entered within it. Some adaptations apparently designed to generate a sense of interactivity may prove little different from the commodified spectacles produced in Hollywood or on Broadway. One especially glaring instance is the videogame of *Fight Club* (2004), which offers an impoverished story-world, fetishizing the bone-crunching aspects of the source-narrative(s) but making little attempt to engage the gamer in a political, as against a merely pugilistic, drama.

Other participatory adaptations, however, may be more liberating in their effects, opening up rather than foreclosing the potentials of the adapted texts. Such interactivity might take the form of 'writing back to' the source-novels. At the most advanced literary level, novelists themselves may 'self-adapt', as when Ellis recycles the figure of Patrick Bateman as a postmodern spectre in *Lunar Park* (2005). In more subterranean reaches of authorship, amateur writers, posting their work online, produce fan fiction that imagines alternative stories emerging from novels they value. Our surfing of FanFiction.net during the composition of this book found, among many such micro-narratives, an extension of *American Psycho* (by 'M. Soames') that neatly conjoins two literary cults by having Bateman disembowel a woman who has the cheek to be ahead of him when queuing for the final Harry Potter novel. Fan fictions in this vein clearly have dialogical and democratizing capacities, both by muting the power of the source-text through vivid reinterpretation and by being available, in turn, for critique and revision by other members of such electronic communities. An element of participatory democracy can also be sensed in the numerous blogs, websites and social networks maintained by fans of contemporary US novelists. Exemplary here are 'The Cult' (a website dedicated to Palahniuk's fiction), 'NotAnExit.net' (an Ellis-related blog) and, more strikingly still, the multiple electronic communities gathered around Mark Z. Danielewski's cult novel, *House of Leaves* (2000), a text that, initially appearing excerpted on the internet, bypassed protocols of mainstream publication.

It is important not to be uncritically celebratory of these recent developments. In the first instance, the frequently submerged, ephemeral existence of websites, blogs and fan fictions responsive to new American fiction means that their power to shape interpretation remains modest compared with that of publishing conglomerates, professionalized media outlets and even academia. Second, these electronic forums sometimes seem less like attractively unruly gatherings than cathedrals in which a preaching to the converted monotonously takes place: 'The Cult', as Palahniuk's most prominent fan site is named, does not sound especially welcoming to an exposé, such as ours above, of the limits of *Fight Club*'s anti-commodity vision. Nevertheless, while remaining cautious, we should acknowledge that these diverse virtual spaces allow less predictable afterlives and adaptations of contemporary American novels to be glimpsed in prototypical form.

CHAPTER EIGHT

CRITICAL CONTEXTS

APPROACHES TO THE CONTEMPORARY AMERICAN NOVEL

The study of the contemporary American novel can and should be refracted through a variety of conceptual prisms. While we should be wary of the dangers of a theoretical free-for-all, a state of affairs in which the diversity of approaches is taken to matter more than their relative strengths and urgencies, it is important to have more than one interpretive paradigm available when reading new fiction from the United States. Underpinning our case studies above, for example, are various Marxisms, feminisms, postcolonial theories and forms of border study. Given a different selection of primary texts, we might have turned productively to other conceptual resources such as 'queer theory' or 'masculinity studies'. In what follows, however, rather than attempting quixotically to cover the whole of this theoretical ground, we describe and evaluate four frameworks that strike us as particularly useful for the study of contemporary US fiction. These analytical approaches are not, of course, self-standing; rather, they have been shaped in dialogues, both friendly and antagonistic, with other intellectual traditions.

Thinking race and ethnicity

'Deep within the word "American" is race', writes Toni Morrison in *Playing in the Dark* (1993: 47). Racial differences and antagonisms are indeed fundamental to the economics, politics and culture of the United States, a nation, after all, that established its territory by genocidal displacement of Native Americans and consolidated its wealth by the labour of diverse non-whites extending from African

Americans in slavery to Chinese immigrants who faced oppressive working conditions on the railroads of the nineteenth century. Even as we write, the still demographically and socially dominant white population is mobilizing military, judicial and political resources against a perceived invasion of South-western states by Mexican incomers. Framed in public discourse as simply an assertion of economic nationalism in hard times, such activity along the US/Mexico border is nevertheless open to reading as an attempt to preserve 'white' land from incursion by Latino/as. This is precisely the kind of racist conceptualization of national space that, in Chapter 5, we saw both documented and resisted by Silko's *Almanac of the Dead*.

Given, as Morrison also says, that 'American means white' (1993: 47), it is unsurprising that the first anthologies and surveys of American literature construed it as exclusively white-authored. Understandably, much energy has subsequently been devoted by minority communities in the United States to defining and entrenching alternative literary traditions that might be endowed with ethnic particularity or distinctness. The positing of bodies of work called, say, *African American literature* or *Native American literature* has proved crucial to the self-affirmation of peoples placed historically in situations of unequal power. Such work is ongoing, not least in the amount of academic activity dedicated to an ethnic segmenting of the contemporary fiction of the US. Typical of this scholarship is Darryl Dickson-Carr's *Columbia Guide to African American Fiction* (2005), which discusses not only a 'high' or 'literary' tradition descending through Morrison, Walker, John Edgar Wideman, Edward P. Jones and others, but also considers how recent black productivity in the novel form has traversed popular genres such as crime writing (numerous figures from Walter Mosley to Valerie Wilson Wesley) or science fiction (Mosley again, along with Octavia Butler). Canon-formation has embraced, as well, the contemporary fiction of other minority communities in the United States. Evidence here would include Ilan Stavans's *Norton Anthology of Latino Literature* (2010), its most recent selections featuring writers such as Junot Díaz and Cristina García; or Guiyou Huang's *Columbia Guide to Asian American Literature Since 1945* (2006), which admits into a body of ethnically particularized fiction such current novelists as Mukherjee, Tan, Maxine Hong Kingston, Chang-rae Lee and Karen Tei Yamashita. There is a progressive intent underlying anthologies and critical compendia like these, acknowledged by John Carlos Rowe when he emphasizes the value of programmes of study 'devoted to the historical specificity and internal development of the diverse communities in the United States' (2002: 14).

Suggestively for us, however, Rowe also registers unease with an ethnically fragmented model of US culture. Despite its laudable aim of promoting the self-realization of vulnerable, historically embattled communities, this dividing-up of cultural production according to race and ethnicity 'risks adopting as its social ideal a simplistic pluralism – every discrete cultural group in the United States deserves its own recognition and study' (2002: 9). Paul Gilroy makes a similar point, more provocatively, when he deplores 'ethnically cleansed canon-building operations' (1993: 145). The sense of 'crossing', the connotations of fluidity rather than fixedness, evoked in the very title of his book, *The Black Atlantic*, indicate his discomfort with accounts of any minority community's literature as stable and sufficient to itself. Far from setting African American literature apart by virtue of its authors' ethnic kinship, Gilroy explores it as a body of work criss-crossed by the tracks of many cultural traditions. Rowe, too, while not wishing prematurely to abandon ethnically particularized literary study, is interested less in theorizing the distinctiveness of the various cultures comprising the US than in redirecting attention towards their entanglements. Thus he takes as his unit of study the 'contact zone', glossing this term as 'the liminal region or border zone in which different cultures meet and negotiate – violently or otherwise – their neighborhood' (2002: 12).

The value of scepticism towards literary nationalisms in the US can be affirmed by returning briefly to several novels discussed in our central chapters. Certainly, there is still evidence there of projections of ethnic autonomy: exemplary might be occasional pronouncements of Indian nationalism in *Almanac of the Dead*, dreams of the decontamination of Native American lands and cultures from the marks of 'the white man'. *Beloved*, too, is, as we saw in Chapter 4, connected by its rage to the radical black nationalisms of Morrison's formative period during the late 1960s. Generically, structurally, even syntactically, however, this novel cannot, in Gilroy's terms, be 'ethnically cleansed': in its recourse to Gothic to disturb the complacencies of the existing racial settlement are debts to nineteenth-century white writers including Edgar Allan Poe and Nathaniel Hawthorne, while in the novel's disjunctive temporality and even in the elasticity of its sentences can be discerned the modernist practice of Virginia Woolf, a novelist much studied by Morrison. *Beloved* is itself, then, a cultural contact zone, defined only inaccurately and clumsily by the language of ethnic particularism. *The Human Stain*, Chapter 4's other case study, offers likewise an exploration of race's fictions and fluidities, if also an acknowledgement of race's traumatizing power in the United States as it has been historically constituted.

Two other conceptual strains should be briefly noted. The first is the emergence, during the past fifteen years, of 'whiteness studies', an analytical mode that aims to deprive ethnic whiteness of its previous invisibility and to correct the state of affairs whereby discussions of race in the United States have historically involved talking about all racial groupings besides the socially dominant one. Whiteness studies shares a progressive project with those forms of identity politics sketched above, yet has a very different methodology, enlisting negative rather than positive energies. While identity politics seeks to raise up, this new analysis of whiteness aspires to tear down. As Steve Garner puts it, the 'initial impetus for theorizing whiteness was an anti-racist recasting of the world through a critique of existing power relations' (2007: 3). That is not to say, however, that the emergence of this new intellectual field has been universally welcomed. Rather like masculinity studies in the age of feminism, whiteness studies in the age of multiculturalism may look suspiciously like the restoration of a discredited subject to centre-stage. As other critics have argued, bringing whiteness into sight and revealing its specific social locations do not amount, in themselves, to an undoing of its privilege. From our narrower perspective, however, it seems clear that whiteness studies can generate productive readings of novels in which, otherwise, race might be occluded as an object for consideration: Marilynne Robinson's *Gilead* (2004), for instance, set in the monochromatic Mid-west of the 1950s.

While practitioners of whiteness studies aim to produce finer-grained versions of 'race-thinking', other theorists propose that this should be done away with altogether. For Walter Benn Michaels, racial discourse in the contemporary US is more harmful than emancipatory: 'the phantasm of respect for difference' has taken the place, he says, of 'commitment to economic justice' (2006: 16).

The case is made with rhetorical flair, even if Michaels tends to model the race/class dynamic as a zero-sum game whereby a prioritizing of race inevitably entails the relegating of class. Approaching race-thinking from another angle, Gilroy is nevertheless as anxious as Michaels to see its decay. He suggests investment instead in 'planetary humanism', conjuring up the vision of 'a fragile, universal humanity powerful enough to make race and ethnicity suddenly meaningless' (2000: 249). This appeal to 'humanity' might seem premature, suspending rather too quickly real-world conditions in the US in which race is still lived out differentially. Valuably for us, however, Gilroy's work also prompts the reflection that American literary study is served only variably by a concern with race and that broader analytical frames are required. We turn now to some recent attempts to supply these.

Border theory and transnational studies

Much ethnically focused work on the literature of the United States has, historically, been *intra*-national in geographical scale. While acknowledging global transits such as the migration of African American writers to France after World War II, it has often been centripetal in its momentum, seeking most energetically to identify and theorize a number of ethnically distinct literatures produced inside the US. Vital though these studies have been in contesting white dominance of the nation, they have tended nevertheless to assume the coherence and authority of the national borders themselves. Yet as Wai Chee Dimock observes, no 'spatial locale' can be granted autonomy from other geographies: 'It is constantly stretched, punctured, and infiltrated. Territorial sovereignty is poor prophylactic' (2006: 4). Thus even the United States, with its quasi-militaristic frontier protection, is not unbreachable, but, rather, is enmeshed in complex relations with numerous other locales. Recent work on US cultural production has, in Dimock's spirit, adjusted the focus from the intra- to the *trans*national, and we wish to survey some of the key insights and problems of this growing body of scholarship.

Particularly in the wake of John Carlos Rowe's 2002 book of the same title, a transnationally oriented approach to the cultures of the US has often been labelled the 'New American Studies'. Like some other claims of intellectual novelty, this one is overstated. Right from its beginnings early in the twentieth century, American Studies displayed, if inconsistently, an international sensibility. Paul Giles reminds us that 'The first American literature group that convened at the Modern Language Association in 1926 maintained that Americanists should not become sidetracked into narrowly nationalistic concerns' (2001: 5). It was not the case that until recent years the discipline was ruled absolutely by exceptionalist thinking, by the notion that the US is sufficient to itself, possessing an essence not sullied by cross-border exchanges. Where the New American Studies *is* new, however, is in radically extending and multiplying the lines that connect the United States to the rest of the world. If earlier work tended to put the US primarily in contact with England, or with other parts of Old Europe, current scholarship is interested in tracing the nation's involvement in an array of hemispheric and global dynamics. Strikingly, critics have recourse to fields such as cybernetics, electronics and neurology for metaphors by which to evoke these proliferating transits and trajectories. For Giles, the literature of the United States should be approached not via 'the old model of a sacred land', but, rather, 'in terms of feedback systems and loops of communication' (2002: 283). For Dimock, the national literature is not an autonomous entity, but, on the contrary, something traversed by 'input channels, kinship networks, routes of transit, and forms of attachment – connective tissues binding America to the rest of the world' (2006: 3).

Although critics working now on the literature of the United States generally consent to the case for transnational reading, they vary considerably in their calculations of geographical scale. Some scholars, as we shall see, make the planet itself the circumference of their discussions; others, however, focus more narrowly on the nation's border territories. Underplaying, in the main, the significance of the northern frontier with Canada, critics have been especially interested in exploring the literature of the borderlands between the United States and Mexico. This particular liminal zone is, according to José David Saldívar, 'a paradigm of crossings, intercultural exchanges, circulations, resistances, and negotiations' (1997: ix). Saldívar and other current border theorists continue to draw on the pioneering intellectual and creative contribution made by the Chicana writer Gloria Anzaldúa in *Borderlands/La Frontera* (1987). Anzaldúa evokes 'an "alien" consciousness [...] a consciousness of the Borderlands', emerging from the 'racial, ideological, cultural and biological cross-pollinization' (1987: 77) that occurs along the US/Mexico line. From its bilingual title onwards, Anzaldúa's book is itself border discourse, ceaselessly crossing between two territorial jurisdictions and between multiple languages (not only formal versions of both English and Spanish, but also their colloquial variants and innovative composites). If subsequent scholars in the United States have elaborated and updated Anzaldúa's cultural cartography, so too have the nation's novelists. As well as *Almanac of the Dead* and *Blood Meridian*, discussed in Chapter 5, border novels from our period include McCarthy's later Border Trilogy (1992–8) and *No Country for Old Men* (2005); texts by many Chicano/a writers, including Rolando Hinojosa, Arturo Islas and John Rechy; and, very recently, William T. Vollmann's encyclopaedic, 1200-page *Imperial* (2009).

Both novelistic and theoretical discourses of the border, however, may still be open to critique. While Anzaldúa is careful to materialize the US/Mexico frontier, alluding to the difficulties as well as opportunities of this terrain for her as a lesbian Chicana, some writers have been less scrupulous, too inclined to figure the border as an exemplary site of fluidity and freedom. Writing in another context, Hamid Naficy cautions that 'metaphorization, multiplication, and shifting of borders are often made productive in postcolonial and multicultural discourses by safely abstracting the borders and by ignoring the unequal power relations there' (2001: 240). Greater weight should be given to the agonies and perils of frontier-crossing, as vividly instantiated along the US/Mexico line at present by the ever-lengthening, highly militarized security fence. Besides an occasional tendency towards abstraction, border theory presents other difficulties. Intended to challenge the power of the United States, its very identification of the nation's marginal spaces may attest perversely to the continuing power of the centre. As Saldívar says, border discourse is 'Janus-faced' (1997: 21), having both progressive and reactionary implications: just as it 'undermines' national authority and 'makes it fragile', so it also '*produces power and reinforces it*' (xiv: emphasis added).

A similar ambivalence attaches to recent attempts to direct transnational study of US literature well beyond the nation's border zones. Some of the most significant work here has been done by Dimock, in both *Through Other Continents* (2006) and her essay, 'Planet and America, Set and Subset' (2007). As these titles themselves suggest,

Dimock proposes less the conceptual abandonment of the nation-state than its recalibration by invoking intercontinental and even planetary levels of significance. Hence, in her words, the literature of the United States should be understood by 'a world atlas of which the national map is inextricably a part' (2007: 8). Important in its humane aspirations, appealing not to narrow national interests but to that 'fragile, universal humanity' imagined by Gilroy, Dimock's globalizing of US literature offers an important resource for the reading of contemporary novels. Some of this fiction is itself explicitly globetrotting, instances of which include William Gibson's *Pattern Recognition* (2003) and Thomas Pynchon's *Against the Day* (2006). Even where novels remain on US soil, the social and cultural spaces they demarcate are now increasingly transnational in status rather than rigorously nationalized. Consider, for example, how the streets of New York City only briefly 'house' both migrant humanity and mobile finance capital in DeLillo's *Cosmopolis* (as discussed in Chapter 6), or how Miami is mapped as a 'World City' in Tom Wolfe's *Back to Blood* (due in 2012).

Even as this transnational or planetary version of American Studies opens up new interpretive possibilities, however, some caution is appropriate. If the discipline is now to define itself by following lines from the United States into an array of global spaces, then this may, dangerously, mimic imperialism's itinerary. There are ominous analogies, too, between the new intercontinental freedoms of such study and the hypermobility of contemporary capital. Dimock herself is sensitive to this danger, noting that 'The drawing of larger and yet larger circles for our discipline can be less than benign [...] indeed, it is an act of self-aggrandizing not unlike the global transactions of capitalism' (2007: 10). The effort required of the New American Studies, then, is greatly to expand its geographical and cultural reach without this taking on the character of imperialistic acquisition.

Postmodernism

In 'Lyotardian Narrative in the works of Pynchon', Wilhelm Bailey proposes that while Lady Gaga's 'Bad Romance' 'affirms capitalist subcultural theory [...] "Alejandro" deconstructs textual situationism' (Bulhak 1996). We would take issue with this, but there is a problem even more pressing than our lack of familiarity with contemporary popular music: neither 'Wilhelm Bailey' nor his essay on Pynchon, strictly speaking, exists. Both were fabricated by an iPhone app called the 'Postmodernism Generator'. This program is based on software written in the mid-90s by Andrew Bulhak to randomly spawn spoofs of academic writing. One of the ironies of calling this software the 'Postmodernism Generator' is that it mirrors many features of the subject it parodies: postmodernism itself is associated with parody and irony; playfulness and plagiarism; challenges to authority and to artistic and academic seriousness; the splicing of high culture and pop culture, of technology and electronic media. Over the past thirty years postmodernism has been the subject of parody, eulogy and fierce debate. Some writers have derided it as the uncritical embrace of the worst aspects of consumer capitalism, while others have welcomed it as liberation from dated modernist paradigms, ushering in a realm of playfulness, reinvention, diversity and difference.

Whatever their particular standpoint, almost all critics agree that postmodernism is tied up with socioeconomic changes and technological developments that have occurred since the Second World War. In broad brushstrokes, we can paint the modernist era, from the late nineteenth to the mid twentieth centuries, as a period revolving around industry and production, factories, fossil fuels and heavy machinery, big cities and bureaucracy. In the postmodern era, since roughly the late 1960s, these modernist features, though still present, have appeared to be eclipsed, with landscapes and lives increasingly shaped by consumerism and the media, by information technology and communication networks, and by digital economies and virtual worlds. Various designations have been used to describe this new order: 'late capitalism' and 'globalization', 'consumer society' and 'postindustrial society', the 'information society' and the 'media society'. 'Postmodernity' is an umbrella term that designates the era in which these changes have occurred and the type of society that has emerged. 'Postmodernism' typically refers to the aesthetic and cultural practices characteristic of this new social formation.

One of the most influential theorists of the postmodern is the French critic Jean Baudrillard (1929–2007). For Baudrillard, media saturation and information overload have resulted in the displacement of reality by a 'hyper-reality' which is 'more-than-real'. The hyper-real is constituted by the glut of signs, images and

THE CONTEMPORARY AMERICAN NOVEL IN CONTEXT

representations generated by omnipresent electronic technologies. In the postmodern world, signs and images no longer copy the real world: they have *become* the real world. Signs in the hyper-real environment of 24/7 TV, cinema, videogames, advertising and the internet refer primarily to each other, and people are now more accustomed to viewing images of things than viewing the thing itself. Virtual reality is not so much a science fiction fantasy of the future as the logic of everyday life in the here-and-now of postmodern society. As we saw in Chapter 3, Baudrillard makes the stunning claim that images have, in effect, 'murdered' the real; reality has been destroyed by spectacles, simulations and simulacra, and everything is now 'a copy of a copy of a copy' (Palahniuk 1999a: 21).

While Baudrillard contends that reality is no longer real, the American theorist Fredric Jameson has associated postmodernism with a range of pathological symptoms including schizophrenia, hysteria, paranoia and the 'waning of affect' (an acute numbing of feeling) that cumulatively express the loss of history and the death of individual identity. For Jameson, postmodernism is not merely one style among others but a 'cultural dominant', reflective of developments in late capitalism whereby culture and all other areas of social life have been systematically penetrated by the market (1991: 4). The subject in this postmodern society is synchronized with the space-time of global capitalism and electronic media, immersed in a 'perpetual present' and consequently cut off from any meaningful sense of the past or the future (178). In our readings above of *Beloved*, *Blood Meridian* and *Oscar Wao*, we saw examples of a self-conscious historical fiction that Linda Hutcheon identifies as prominent in the postmodern era. For Jameson, however, the postmodern novel, like postmodern culture more broadly, is afflicted with 'historical deafness' (xi). In a close reading of E. L. Doctorow's novel *Ragtime* (1975), he insists that:

> This historical novel can no longer set out to represent the historical past; it can only 'represent' our ideas and stereotypes about that past (which thereby at once becomes 'pop history') [...] we are condemned to seek History by way of our own pop images and simulacra of that history, which itself remains forever out of reach. (33)

Jameson is not alone among critics of the postmodern in finding the historical imagination atrophied throughout the public and private spheres. History has been colonized by a nostalgia industry and reduced to a supermarket of 'styles'. The past becomes little more than an image in a retro film (Jameson offers Polanski's neo-noir *Chinatown* (1974) as an example), or in a line of clothing, a tourist photo opportunity or a themed restaurant. According to this critique, not only public history but private memories, also, are increasingly commodified by capital and shaped by mnemonic technology. Lost amidst sensory experiences of the present, the postmodern subject forfeits coherence and continuity over time and becomes a plastic or even, according to Jameson, a 'schizophrenic' entity (1991: 10).

While modernist works are generally regarded as serious and sincere, profound and original, postmodern texts tend to be playful and ironic, wilfully depthless and superficial, privileging style over substance. Jameson invokes Edvard Munch's painting *The Scream* (1893) as 'the canonical expression of the great modernist thematics of alienation, anomie, solitude, social fragmentation and isolation' (19). Postmodernism, however, might be exemplified by the horror-film spoof *Scream* (1996). In Wes Craven's movie, a serial killer wears a mask echoing Munch's painting, and this intertextual allusion is only one among many in a work also packed with references to other horror films. Further features of the postmodern are suggested here. While modernism sought to repel mass culture, postmodernism incorporates it, undoing distinctions between 'high' and 'low' art. Postmodern texts are often hyperbolically self-referential: Bret Easton Ellis's *Lunar Park* (2005), for example, not only features a guest appearance by Patrick Bateman from *American Psycho* but knowingly constructs its own horror narrative from an inventory of clichés from the fiction of Stephen King. For Jameson, such texts illustrate the postmodern preference for pastiche – a blank imitation or recycling of aesthetic forms – as opposed to the satirical and critical impulses that drive parody.

A key part of the self-reflexivity and hyperactive intertextuality of postmodern art is the mixing of genres and styles. In Jameson's account, postmodernism revolves around the 'random cannibalization of all the styles of the past, the play of random stylistic allusion' (1991: 26). Like channel-hopping on TV or surfing the Net, postmodern art produces jarring jump-cuts and juxtapositions as it flicks between generic codes. In *Against the Day*, for example, Pynchon weaves a patchwork pastiche out of writings of the late nineteenth-century *fin-de-siècle* era in which it is set: the pulp westerns of Zane Grey; the science fiction of Jules Verne and H. G. Wells; the Victorian Gothic of Bram Stoker; the adventure stories of the Hardy Boys; the spy fiction of Joseph Conrad and John Buchan; the exploration memoirs of Henry Morton Stanley; and the erotic adventures of Leopold von Sacher-Masoch. These genre shifts are accompanied by wild modulations in tone so that the reader is bumped between passages of scientific sobriety (theories of light), pornography (hardcore three-way sex scenes), slapstick comedy (eluding an avalanche of mayonnaise) and apocalyptic horror (the battlefields of the Great War). Díaz's *Oscar Wao*, discussed in Chapter 5, offers, albeit on a smaller scale, a similar pasting and pastiching of multiple genres.

Today, some critics would argue that postmodernism no longer resonates as the 'spirit of the age'. Starting in the 1990s, then intensifying in the wake of the 9/11 attacks in 2001, there has been a discernible turn away from 'play' and 'irony' towards 'history', 'trauma' and 'terror'. Some critics posit the emergence of a 'New Sincerity' and 'post-postmodernism'. As noted in our chapter on globalization, 'postmodernism' was *the* academic buzzword of the 80s and early 90s when the critical scene was inundated with texts on postmodern fiction and poetry, film and television, music and fashion, politics and philosophy, architecture and cities. But although the question today might be less 'what *is*' and more 'what *was*' postmodernism, it remains a key word in the critical vocabulary of anyone interested in the contemporary American novel.

Ecocriticism

'Postmodernism is what you have', writes Fredric Jameson, 'when the modernization process is complete and nature is gone for good' (1991: ix). With the natural liquidated, culture itself becomes a 'veritable "second nature"' (ix). Jameson's vision has a sci-fi quality, evoking a world in which the sensory richness of landscape, the manifold array of flora and fauna, persist only as memories or simulacra. Indeed, his work has value as a theoretical companion to achievements in contemporary American science fiction. Take, for example, the famous opening sentence of William Gibson's *Neuromancer* (1984), which reverses the traditional order of priority between nature and culture, between unmediated experience and the apparatus of mediation: 'The sky above the port was the color of television, tuned to a dead channel' (1997: 3). Many other novels not usually parcelled up with SF have also, in varying moods of dread and exhilaration, mapped the contemporary United States according to Jameson's thesis of the postmodern death of the natural. In one of several rhapsodies to the supermarket in DeLillo's *White Noise* (1985), the lustre of a natural product is understood as derived from that of its mediated version which, again, takes conceptual precedence: 'The fruit was gleaming and wet, hard-edged. There was a self-conscious quality about it. It looked carefully observed, like four-color fruit in a guide to photography' (1986: 170).

Nature might indeed appear 'gone for good' in the US of today, with its ever-expanding urban sprawls, its dominant architectures of the mall and the superhighway, its saturation by advanced technologies of mediation and replication such as the computer, the cell-phone, the iPod. And yet what Jameson terms 'the modernization process' is evidently incomplete: nature continues, stubbornly, to make its presence felt. In front of us as we write is the latest copy (14 August 2010) of one of America's leading newspapers, the *Los Angeles Times*. The paper's lead story concerns the impact on fragile ecologies along the coast of the Gulf of Mexico of the catastrophic spillage from BP's oil rig, the *Deepwater Horizon*. Environmental anxiety is sounded, too, in an article on the approval of 'genetically engineered salmon' for consumption in the United States. But the pleasures, rather than crises, of non-human nature are apparent in other pieces, such as that headed 'National parks, forests to waive entry fees this weekend'. If it is the case that the natural is not apprehended spontaneously, but is irrevocably framed by prior knowledges and vocabularies, that is not grounds for querying its materiality. Far from being annihilated by postmodernity, nature endures, its present condition a matter of urgent inquiry for discourses and disciplines that include, not least, the literary and the literary-critical.

'Ecocriticism', developing in the US and elsewhere during the past two decades, aims precisely to explore the literary modelling of relations between human and non-human natures. This critical field is, however, variegated, contentious, even contradictory. Lacking, in Lawrence Buell's words, a 'paradigm-defining statement', it is primarily 'issue-driven' and 'gathers itself around a commitment to environmentality from whatever critical vantage point' (2005: 11). If ecocritics share common ground in investigating human impacts upon ecosystems as registered by literary texts, they differ in many other respects. While some scholars discuss literary representations of landscape, others explore how texts of various kinds either contribute to, or thwart, sustainable relationships between humans and non-human species. Ecocritics clash, too, in political philosophy: a number may be ideologically quiescent, wanting to preserve delicate ecosystems in their present state and differing thereby from others who see such models of harmony as building in inequalities of classes, genders and races. The scale of ecocritical analysis also varies. Much work in this vein is focused upon the local, on elaborating how literary texts delineate particular landscapes in the United States. But ecocritics may also work to macroscopic specification, mimicking the New American Studies discussed earlier by moving outwards from the local to the bioregional, the continental and, ultimately, the planetary. Buell cites instances of late twentieth-century studies linked by a 'common thread of conceiving the United States as connected to or impinging upon far-distant lands via its environmentality, whether this be its groves, its uranium, or its garbage' (2007: 234). The middle item in Buell's list is very apt here, given the linkage we saw Silko making in *Almanac of the Dead* between the depredations of uranium mining in New Mexico and the devastating atomic air-raids upon Japan.

To some critics, however, contemporary US fiction suffers from a lack of ecological imagination. Scott Russell Sanders argues that it has 'an indoor cast' of mind (1996: 194). Yet this diagnosis of novelistic agoraphobia is contestable on two counts. First, he neglects numerous counter-examples: we have discussed in detail the South-western literary landscaping of McCarthy and Silko, two writers minutely sensitive to geographical, geological, botanical and zoological particularities. To their work can be added that of other environmentalists of the current US novel, including Ursula K. Le Guin, Annie Proulx and Alice Walker. These female names should not be taken to imply, by some reconfigured division of sexual labour, that ecology is for females only; nevertheless, all three writers explore, in ecofeminist fashion, the structural connections in the United States between exploitations of nature and of women.

There is a second reason to dispute Sanders's analysis of an impoverished environmental consciousness in contemporary American fiction. Buell records that ecocriticism itself has lately turned away from exclusive concern with 'the literatures of nature and preservationist environmentalism' and developed an interest, too, in representations of 'metropolitan and/or toxified landscapes' (2005: viii). His own volume, *Writing for an Endangered World* (2001) includes studies not only of texts traditionally designated 'nature writing' but of contemporary urban fiction, such as the African American novelist John Edgar Wideman's explorations of a degraded zone of Philadelphia in his Homewood Trilogy (1981–3). In similar vein, Tom Lynch writes that ecocriticism should look in previously unexplored literary works for 'a somatic and sensuous semiotics in which the full range of human senses engage in the experience of place' (2008: 184). One project on such reroutings of ecological sensibility into the urban, we suggest, might involve studying elements of the post-9/11 novel, such as the registering of vulnerable ecosystems in New York City in Joseph O'Neill's *Netherland* (2008).

We began this chapter by both recommending a plurality of critical approaches to contemporary American fiction and cautioning against its dangers. As it happens, ecocritics are among those scholars most anxious about a wasteful proliferation of methods, with William Rueckert arguing that 'there must be a shift in our locus of motivation from newness, or theoretical elegance, or even coherence, to a principle of relevance' (1996: 106–7). Lynch, too, has 'relevance' in mind, an urgently felt connection between theoretical commitment and material practice, when he notes that 'there are few ecocritics who are not also, in at least modest ways, ecoactivists as well' (2008: 230). Indeed, we might query his implied distinction here and suggest that studying literary ecologies – not least the literary ecologies produced in the nation which remains the world's most extravagant consumer – is itself an ecoactivist act. But ecocritics are not alone in attempting to fashion continuities between life inside and life outside the university seminar room. As we hope to have shown in this book, critics who approach the contemporary American novel from a wide variety of engaged standpoints are themselves, 'in at least modest ways', activists, participating intensely in a dialogue about the meanings and directions of the United States.

REVIEW, READING AND RESEARCH

Chapter 7: Afterlives and Adaptations

Review

- Commercial American cinema has, from its inception, sought to remedy its own 'vulgar' standing by adapting literary works. This attempt by film to borrow literature's 'cultural capital' continues today.
- Novels, including contemporary American novels, are especially appealing to Hollywood as ready-made narratives; they also have already-assembled fan communities who will be interested in seeing them adapted to film.
- While carefully examining film adaptations' reworking of their source-novels, we should recognize that these films also cannibalize many other cultural materials (such as other movies).
- The screen adaptations of *American Psycho*, *Fight Club*, *Beloved* and *The Human Stain* offer these novels a valuable afterlife, but, at times, through their formal and narrative selections, deflect the novels' transgressive power.
- In our digital era, adaptation of novels may take many other forms besides transposition to the big screen: e.g. the more 'participatory' formats of videogames, fan fictions, author-related blogs and social networking sites.

Reading

Cartmell, D. and Whelehan, I. (2010), *Screen Adaptation: Impure Cinema*. Basingstoke: Palgrave Macmillan.

Hutcheon, L. (2006), *A Theory of Adaptation*. New York: Routledge.

Jenkins, H. (2006), *Convergence Culture: Where Old and New Media Collide*. New York: New York University Press.

Palmer, R. B. (ed.) (2007), *Twentieth-Century American Fiction on Screen*. Cambridge: Cambridge University Press.

Sanders, J. (2006), *Adaptation and Appropriation*. Abingdon: Routledge.

Stam, R. and Raengo, A. (eds) (2005), *Literature and Film: A Guide to the Theory and Practice of Film Adaptation*. Malden, MA: Blackwell.

Research

- Chapter 7 discusses the film adaptations of four contemporary American novels. Produce case studies of your own by exploring how other works of post-1980 American fiction have been adapted for cinema. What changes are made to the narrative systems and thematic priorities of the source-novels, and with what ideological consequences?

- Take any contemporary American novelist and trace responses to and adaptations of his or her work made electronically by bloggers, fan clubs and writers of fan fiction. What is the effect of these new media platforms upon authorship and authority? Exactly how empowering or democratizing for readers are they?

Chapter 8: Critical Contexts

Review

- While being wary of a relativistic piling-up of multiple critical approaches, we should draw upon a variety of conceptual resources when studying the contemporary American novel.
- Conceptualizations of race, forms of border and transnational study, models of postmodernism, and ecocriticism: all are found by the chapter to be especially productive for reading contemporary American fiction. Each of these theoretical fields, however, is revealed to be internally conflicted and disputatious, rather than blandly consensual. If each conceptual approach is insightful with regard to the primary texts we are studying here, each also has its form of blindness, its problematical assumptions and protocols.
- To read contemporary American fiction from an engaged critical standpoint is not simply to produce rarefied academic discourse but to participate actively in ongoing debate about what the United States is and where it is headed.

Reading

Buell, L. (2005), *The Future of Environmental Criticism: Environmental Crisis and Literary Imagination.* Malden, MA: Blackwell.
—(2007), 'Ecoglobalist affects: the emergence of US environmental imagination on a planetary scale', in W. C. Dimock and L. Buell (eds), *Shades of the Planet: American Literature as World Literature.* Princeton: Princeton University Press, pp. 227–48.
Dimock, W. C. (2006), *Through Other Continents: American Literature Across Deep Time.* Princeton: Princeton University Press.

—(2007), 'Introduction: planet and America, set and subset', in W. C. Dimock and L. Buell (eds), *Shades of the Planet: American Literature as World Literature*. Princeton : Princeton University Press, pp. 1–16.

Dyer, R. (1997), *White: Essays on Race and Culture*. London: Routledge.

Garner, S. (2007), *Whiteness: An Introduction*. Abingdon: Routledge.

Giles, P. (2002), *Virtual Americas: Transnational Fictions and the Transatlantic Imaginary*. Durham, NC: Duke University Press.

—(2011), *The Global Remapping of American Literature*. Princeton: Princeton University Press.

Gilroy, P. (2000), *Between Camps: Nations, Cultures and the Allure of Race*. London: Penguin.

Hutcheon, L. (1989), *The Politics of Postmodernism* London: Routledge.

Lynch, T. (2008), *Xerophilia: Ecocritical Explorations in Southwestern Literature*. Lubbock, TX: Texas Tech University Press.

Michaels, W. B. (2006), *The Trouble with Diversity: How We Learned to Love Identity and Ignore Inequality*. New York: Metropolitan.

Rowe, J. C. (2002), *The New American Studies*. Minneapolis: University of Minnesota Press.

Rueckert, W. (1996), 'Literature and ecology: an experiment in ecocriticism', in C. Glotfelty and H. Fromm (eds), *The Ecocriticism Reader: Landmarks in Literary Ecology*. Athens, GA: University of Georgia Press, pp. 105–23.

Sanders, S. R. (1996), 'Speaking a word for nature', in C. Glotfelty and H. Fromm (eds), *The Ecocriticism Reader: Landmarks in Literary Ecology*. Athens, GA: University of Georgia Press, pp. 182–95.

Siemerling, W. (2005), *The New North American Studies: Culture, Writing and the Politics of Re/Cognition*. Abingdon: Routledge.

Note that additional resources are listed in Part Two's 'Review, Reading and Research': the Chapter 3 bibliography cites key texts on postmodernism by Annesley, Baudrillard and Jameson; the Chapter 4 bibliography cites an array of sources on conceptualizations of race in the US; and that for Chapter 5 lists important work by Anzaldúa, Huhndorf, Newman and Saldívar in the mode of transnational studies.

Research

- Chapter 8 has discussed in detail four particular approaches to contemporary American fiction. Consider whether these critical models might be *combined* in the reading of particular novels, or whether that would be to reveal tension or incompatibility between them: e.g. can a racially oriented reading be articulated with an ecocritical one?

- Research another conceptual resource not considered at length here and evaluate its productivity for a reading of particular American novels: e.g. what happens to Marilynne Robinson's *Home* (2008) when it is seen through the prism of *queer theory*; or to Jane Smiley's *A Thousand Acres* (1991) when read through *masculinity studies*; or to Jonathan Safran Foer's *Everything is Illuminated* (2002) when a *narratological* reading is prioritized?
- Test the strength of our concluding argument that to engage keenly with current American fiction is not a dry-as-dust academic exercise but itself an act charged with political significance.

Additional works cited

Appadurai, A. (1990), 'Disjuncture and difference in the global cultural economy'. *Theory, Culture & Society* 7, 295–310.

—(2001), 'Grassroots globalization and the research imagination', in A. Appadurai (ed.), *Globalization*. Durham, NC: Duke University Press, pp. 1–21.

Appiah, A. (1996), 'Race, culture, identity: misunderstood connections'. *The Tanner Lectures on Human Values* 17: 51–136.

Augé, M. (1995). *Non-Places: Introduction to an Anthropology of Supermodernity*. London: Verso.

Barber, B. (2007), *Consumed: How Capitalism Corrupts Children, Infantilizes Adults, and Swallows Citizens Whole*. New York: Norton.

Barthes, R. (1984), *'Writing Degree Zero' & 'Elements of Semiology'*, trans. A. Lavers and C. Smith. London: Jonathan Cape.

Bauman, Z. (1998), *Globalization: The Human Consequences*. Oxford: Blackwell.

—(2001), *The Individualized Society*. Oxford: Blackwell.

Bell, V. E. (2000), 'Counter-chronicling and alternative mapping in *Memoria del fuego* and *Almanac of the Dead*.' *MELUS* 25, 3–4: 5–30.

Benjamin, W. (1968), *Illuminations: Essays and Reflections*, H. Arendt (ed.), H. Zohn (trans.). New York: Schocken Books.

—(2004), *Selected Writings: Volume 1: 1913–1926*. Cambridge, MA: Belknap Press.

Bourdieu, P. (2003), *Counterfire: Against the Tyranny of the Market*. London: Verso.

Brewton, V. (2004), 'The changing landscape of violence in Cormac McCarthy's early novels and the Border Trilogy'. *Southern Literary Journal* 37, 1: 121–43.

Buell, L. (2001), *Writing for an Endangered World: Literature, Culture, and Environment in the U.S. and beyond*. Cambridge, MA : Belknap Press of Harvard University Press

—(2007), 'Ecoglobalist affects: the emergence of US environmental imagination on a planetary scale', in W. C. Dimock and L. Buell (eds), *Shades of the Planet: American Literature as World Literature*. Princeton: Princeton University Press, pp. 227–48.

Bulhak, A. (1996), *The Postmodernism Generator*. http://www.elsewhere. org/pomo/.

Cairncross, F. (1997), *The Death of Distance: How the Communications Revolution Will Change Our Lives*. Cambridge, MA: Harvard Business Press.

Carter-Sanborn, K. (1994), '"We Murder Who We Were": *Jasmine* and the violence of identity'. *American Literature* 66, 3: 573–93.

Céspedes, D, and S. Torres-Saillant (2000), 'Fiction is the poor man's cinema: an interview with Junot Díaz'. *Callaloo* 23, 2: 892–907.

Coupland, D. (1996), *Generation X: Tales for an Accelerated Culture*. London: Abacus, (first published 1991)

Crosthwaite, P. (2008), 'Fiction in the age of the global accident: Don

DeLillo's *Cosmopolis'*. *The London Consortium: Static.* 7: 1–13, http://static.londonconsortium.com/issue07/05_Crosthwaite_essay.pdf.

Crouch, S. (1987), 'Aunt Medea'. *The New Republic* 197, 16: 38–43.

Davis, M. (2000), *Magical Urbanism: Latinos Reinvent the US Big City.* London: Verso.

DeLillo, D. (1986), *White Noise.* London: Picador (first published 1985).

Eldridge, D. (2008), 'The generic *American Psycho'*. *Journal of American Studies* 42, 1: 19–33.

Eriksen, T. H. (2007), *Globalization: The Key Concepts.* New York: Berg.

Ewen, S. (1990), *All Consuming Images: The Politics of Style in Contemporary Culture.* New York: Basic Books.

Fitzgerald, F. S. (2009), *The Crack-Up.* New York: New Directions (first published 1936).

Fortune 500. 2010. http://money.cnn.com/magazines/fortune/fortune500/2010/.

Freud, S. (2006), 'Mourning and melancholia', in A. Phillips (ed.), *The Penguin Freud Reader.* London: Penguin, pp. 310–26.

GCIM (Global Commission on International Migration) (2005), http://www.gcimorg/attachements/GCIM%20Report%20Synopsis.pdf.

Gibson, W. (1997), *Neuromancer.* New York: Ace Books (first published 1984).

Giddens. A. (2003), *Runaway World. How Globalization is Reshaping our Lives.* New York: Routledge.

Giles, P. (2001), *Transatlantic Insurrections: British Culture and the Formation of American Literature, 1730–1860.* Philadelphia: University of Pennsylvania Press.

Graham, S. (2005), 'Re-reading Leslie Marmon Silko's *Almanac of the Dead* after 9/11'. *English Studies in Africa* 48, 2: 75–88.

Grewal, G. (1993), 'Born again American: the immigrant consciousness in *Jasmine'*, in E. S. Nelson (ed), *Bharati Mukherjee: Critical Perspectives.* New York: Garland. 181–96.

Grewal, I. (1994), 'The postcolonial, ethnic studies, and the diaspora: the contexts of ethnic immigrant/migrant cultural studies in the US'. *Socialist Review* 24, 4: 45–74.

Harley, J. B. (1988), 'Maps, knowledge, and power', in D Cosgrove and S. Daniels (eds), *The Iconography of Landscape: Essays on the Symbolic Representation, Design and Use of Past Environments.* Cambridge: Cambridge University Press, pp. 277–312.

Harris, M. (ed.) (1974), *The Black Book.* New York: Random House.

Harvey, D. (1989), *The Condition of Postmodernity.* Oxford: Basil Blackwell.

Hawthorne, J. (2007), *Confessions and Criticisms.* New York: BiblioBazaar (first published 1887).

Henderson, M. G. (1999), 'Toni Morrison's *Beloved*. Re-membering the body as historical text', in W. L. Andrews and N. Y. McKay (eds), *Toni Morrison's Beloved: A Casebook.* New York: Oxford University Press, pp. 79–106.

Jackson, P., Crang, P. and Dwyer, C. (2004), 'Introduction: the spaces of transnationality', in P. Jackson, P. Crang and C. Dwyer (eds), *Transnational Spaces*. Abingdon: Routledge, pp. 1–23.

James, N. 2000. 'Sick city boy.' *Sight and Sound*. http://www.bfi.org.uk/sightandsound/feature/89.

Jameson, F. (1981), *The Political Unconscious: Narrative as a Socially Symbolic Act*. London: Methuen.

Jefferson, T. (1977), *The Portable Thomas Jefferson*, M. D. Peterson (ed.). New York: Penguin.

Karenga, R. (1968). 'Black Cultural Nationalism'. *Negro Digest* 13, 3: 5–9.

Klein, N. (2007), *The Shock Doctrine: The Rise of Disaster Capitalism*. New York: Metropolitan Books.

Koshy, S. (1998), 'The geography of female subjectivity: ethnicity, gender, and diaspora', in L. P. Zamora (ed.), *Contemporary American Women Writers: Gender, Class, Ethnicity*. London: Longman.

Kunkel, B. (2010), 'Into the big tent'. *London Review of Books* 32, 8: 12–16.

Lasch, C. (1985), *The Minimal Self: Psychic Survival in Troubled Times*. London: Pan Books.

Lash, S. (2007), 'Capitalism and metaphysics'. *Theory, Culture & Society* 24, 5: 1-26.

Marx, K. (1973), *Grundrisse: Foundations of the Critique of Political Economy*. London: Penguin.

—(1993), *The Eighteenth Brumaire of Louis Bonaparte*, in E. Kamenka (ed.), *The Portable Karl Marx*. Harmondsworth: Penguin.

Mask, M. (2005), '*Beloved*: the adaptation of an American slave narrative', in R. Stam and A. Raengo (eds), *Literature and Film: A Guide to the Theory and Practice of Film Adaptation*. Malden, MA: Blackwell, pp. 272–94.

McCarthy, C. (2006), *The Road*. London: Picador.

Milton, J. (1980), *The Complete Poems*, G. Campbell (ed.). London: Dent.

Naficy, H. (2001), *An Accented Cinema: Exilic and Diasporic Filmmaking*. Princeton: Princeton University Press.

O'Brien, R. (1992), *Global Financial Integration: The End of Geography*. London: Chatham House Papers.

Owens, B. (2000), *Cormac McCarthy's Western Novels*. Tucson: University of Arizona Press.

Palahniuk, C. (1999b), 'A chat about the novel *Fight Club*'. CNN interview. http://edition.cnn.com/COMMUNITY/transcripts/palahniuk.html.

Paasonen, S. (ed.) (2007), *Pornification: Sex and Sexuality in Media Culture*. Oxford: Berg.

Radway, J. (2002), 'What's in a name?', in D. E. Pease and R. Wiegman (eds), *The Futures of American Studies*. Durham, NC: Duke University Press, pp. 45–75.

Root, D. (1996), *Cannibal Culture: Art, Appropriation and the Commodification of Difference*. Boulder, CO: Westview Press.

Roppolo, K. (2007), 'Vision, voice, and intertribal metanarrative: the American Indian visual-rhetorical tradition and Leslie Marmon Silko's *Almanac of the Dead*.' *American Indian Quarterly* 31, 4: 534–58.

Rosenblatt, R (1990), 'Snuff this book! Will Bret Easton Ellis get away with murder?' *New York Times*. December 16.

Rowe, J. C. (2007), 'Culture, US imperialism, and globalization', in A. Dawson and M. J. Schueller (eds), *Exceptional State: Contemporary US Culture and the New Imperialism*. Durham, NC: Duke University Press, pp. 37–59.

Said, E. (2001), 'Globalizing literary study'. *PMLA* 116.1: 64–8.

Seltzer, M. (1998), *Serial Killers: Death and Life in America's Wound Culture*. New York: Routledge.

Shaw, J. I. (2008), 'Evil empires: *Blood Meridian*, war in El Salvador, and the burdens of omniscience'. *Southern Literary Journal* 40, 2: 207–31.

Silko, L. M. (1996), *Yellow Woman and a Beauty of the Spirit: Essays on Native American Life Today*. New York: Simon & Schuster.

Strange, S. (1997), *Casino Capitalism*. Manchester: Manchester University Press.

Sultana, R. (2004), 'Mimics without menace: interrogating hybridity in Bharati Mukherjee's fiction', in R. B. H. Goh and S. Wong (eds), *Asian Diasporas: Cultures, Identities, Representations*. Hong Kong: Hong Kong University Press.

Taubin, A. (1999), 'So good it hurts'. *Sight and Sound*. http://www.bfi.org.uk/sightandsound/feature/193/.

Travis, T. (2007), '"It will change the world if everybody reads this book": new thought religion in Oprah's book club.' *American Quarterly*, 59, 3: 1017–41.

Virilio, P. (2003), *Unknown Quantity*. New York: Thames & Hudson.

World Tourism Organization. 2010. http://www.unwto.org/facts/menu.html.

Žižek, S. (2008), *Violence: Six Sideways Reflections*. London: Profile.

INDEX